Table of Conten

M000207831

continued on next page

0-88012-487-3

continued from previous page

STEP FOUR: BEGINNING GEOMETRY

0-88012-487-3

Signed Numbers

Find the Sums

To find the sum of two or more positive integers, add the absolute values and write the sum as a positive integer.

3 + 4 = 7

2 + 6 =

9 + 7 =

6 + 1 =

11 + 6 =

6 + 3 =

To find the sum of two or more negative integers, add the absolute values and write the sum as a negative integer.

(⁻3) + (⁻4) = (⁻7)

(⁻2) + (⁻6) =

(⁻9) + (⁻7) =

(⁻6) + (⁻1) =

(⁻11) + (⁻6) =

(⁻6) + (⁻3) =

7 + 6 + 8 + 2 =

(⁻7) + (⁻6) + (⁻8) + (⁻2) =

6 + 4 + 9 + 3 =

(⁻6) + (⁻4) + (⁻9) + (⁻3) =

Begin Step 1 Signed Numbers

0-88012-487-3

Signed Numbers

Find the Sums

To find the sum of a positive integer and a negative integer, find the difference of the absolute value of the integers and use the sign of the greater integer.

$8 + (^{-}2) = 6$ $\qquad$ $(^{-}8) + 2 = (^{-}6)$

$5 + (^{-}4) =$ $\qquad$ $(^{-}5) + 4 =$

$8 + (^{-}5) =$ $\qquad$ $(^{-}8) + 5 =$

$(^{-}7) + 10 =$ $\qquad$ $7 + (^{-}10) =$

$(^{-}11) + 3 =$ $\qquad$ $11 + (^{-}3) =$

$3 + (^{-}7) =$ $\qquad$ $(^{-}3) + 7 =$

$(^{-}12) + 10 =$ $\qquad$ $12 + (^{-}10) =$

$7 + (^{-}12) =$ $\qquad$ $(^{-}7) + 12 =$

$(^{-}8) + 15 =$ $\qquad$ $8 + (^{-}15) =$

$4 + (^{-}2) =$ $\qquad$ $(^{-}4) + 2 =$

0-88012-487-3

Number Sentences

Fill the blanks so that all the number sentences are true.

				4	+	(-6)	=	
				+				+
(-11)	+		=	(-9)				(-3)
—				=				=
(-8)		12	+		=			
=		—				+		
		(-8)		22	+	(-20)	=	
		=				=		—
			+	(-33)	=			(-10)
								=
				8	—	(-4)	=	

 0-88012-487-3

Signed Numbers

Find the Sums

To find the sum of more than two integers with unlike signs, combine the absolute values of the integers having like signs.

Then combine the total of the positive integers with the total of the negative integers.

Here's how

$1 + (^{-}2) + 4 + (^{-}6) = 5 + (^{-}8) = (^{-}3)$

$5 + (^{-}3) + 2 + (^{-}1) = 7 + (^{-}4) =$

$(^{-}2) + 4 + 3 + (^{-}3) =$

$3 + 2 + (^{-}2) + (^{-}3) =$

$6 + (^{-}2) + (^{-}1) + (^{-}3) =$

$(^{-}3) + (^{-}1) + 2 + 1 =$

$4 + 7 + (^{-}1) + (^{-}3) =$

$6 + 3 + 1 + (^{-}2) =$

$3 + (^{-}3) + (^{-}3) + (^{-}2) =$

0-88012-487-3

Signed Numbers

Find the Sums

To find the sum of more than two integers with unlike signs, combine the absolute values of the integers having like signs.

Then combine the total of the positive integers with the total of the negative integers.

$$3 + (^{-}4) + (^{-}3) + 2 = 5 + (^{-}7) = (^{-}2)$$

$2 + (^{-}1) + 4 + (^{-}3) = 6 + (^{-}4) =$

$(^{-}1) + (^{-}5) + 2 + 3 =$

$4 + (^{-}2) + (^{-}2) + (^{-}3) =$

$(^{-}6) + 3 + (^{-}2) + 6 =$

$(^{-}5) + 2 + (^{-}5) + 1 =$

$6 + 2 + (^{-}3) + 3 =$

$7 + (^{-}3) + (^{-}4) + 1 =$

$1 + (^{-}3) + (^{-}3) + 1 =$

0-88012-487-3

Signed Numbers

Find the Differences

To find the difference between two integers having unlike signs, change the sign of the integer which is being subtracted, and find the sum.

$5 - (^{-}1) =$
$5 + 1 = 6$

$(^{-}5) - 1 =$
$(^{-}5) + (^{-}1) = {}^{-}6$

$(^{-}5) - (^{-}1) =$
$(^{-}5) + 1 = (^{-}4)$

$5 - 1 =$
$5 + (^{-}1) = 4$

$3 - (^{-}8) =$

$(^{-}3) - (^{-}8) =$

$(^{-}3) - 8 =$

$3 - 8 =$

$(^{-}7) - (^{-}6) =$

$(^{-}7) - 6 =$

$7 - (^{-}6) =$

$7 - 6 =$

0-88012-487-3

Number Sentences

Fill the blanks so that all the number sentences are true.

(-3)				(-10)	—	11	=	
+				+				
(-4)	+	4	=					
=				=				
					+	6	=	
						—		+
				(-15)		(-4)		
				+		=		=
		(-4)	+	14	=			0
		—						
		(-4)			—	(-8)	=	
		=						

 0-88012-487-3

Signed Numbers

Find the Differences

To find the difference between two integers having unlike signs, change the sign of the integer which is being subtracted, and find the sum.

$9 - (^{-}2) =$
$9 + 2 = 11$

$(^{-}9) - (^{-}2) =$
$(^{-}9) + 2 = {}^{-}7$

$(^{-}9) - 2 =$
$(^{-}9) + (^{-}2) = {}^{-}11$

$9 - (^{-}2) =$
$9 + 2 = 11$

$4 - (^{-}10) =$

$(^{-}4) - 10 =$

$(^{-}4) - (^{-}10) =$

$4 - 10 =$

$(^{-}15) - 8 =$

$(^{-}15) - (^{-}8) =$

$15 - 8 =$

$15 - (^{-}8) =$

0-88012-487-3

Tic-Tac-Toe

Combine the signed numbers. Write the answers in the corresponding spaces on the square below.

a. (-12) + 8 =

b. (-6) — (-12) =

c. (-12) + 4 =

d. (-13) — (-7) =

e. (-8) + 6 =

f. (-6) — (-8) =

g. 2 — (-2) =

h. (-4) + (-6) =

i. (-8) — (-8) =

a.	b.	c.
d.	e.	f.
g.	h.	i.

Add every row, every column, and both diagonals. If your answers are correct, all totals will be the same.

0-88012-487-3

Signed Numbers

Signed Numbers

Perform the operations indicated.

$5 + 9 =$ $\qquad$ $(^-5) + (^-11) =$

$(^-12) + (^-6) =$ $\qquad$ $3 + (^-8) =$

$4 + (^-7) =$ $\qquad$ $12 + (^-7) =$

$(^-9) + 10 =$ $\qquad$ $10 + (^-4) =$

$8 + (^-10) =$ $\qquad$ $(^-10) - (^-14) =$

$(^-12) - (^-8) =$ $\qquad$ $(^-13) - (+10) =$

$12 - (^-6) =$ $\qquad$ $6 - (^-15) =$

$9 + (^-12) + 15 + (^-16) =$

0-88012-487-3

Tic-Tac-Toe

Combine the signed numbers. Write the answers in the corresponding spaces on the square below.

a. (-15) + 14 =

b. (-2) + 11 =

c. (-6) + 1 =

d. (-7) + 4 =

e. 5 + (-4) =

f. (-4) + 9 =

g. 4 — (-3) =

h. (-6) + (-1) =

i. (-8) + 11 =

a.	b.	c.
d.	e.	f.
g.	h.	i.

Add every row, every column, and both diagonals. If your answers are correct, all totals will be the same.

0-88012-487-3

Signed Numbers

Find the Products

The product of two integers with like signs is a positive integer equal to the product of the factors.

$6 \cdot 8 = 48$

$(^-5)(^-7) = 35$

$3 \cdot 4 =$

$(^-8)(^-9) =$

$(^-4)(^-7) =$

$6 \cdot 4 =$

$3 \cdot 7 =$

$(^-3)(^-12) =$

$8 \cdot 10 =$

$(^-6)(^-9) =$

The product of two integers with unlike signs is a negative integer equal to the product of the factors.

$(^-6)8 = (^-48)$

$5(^-7) = (^-35)$

$3(^-4) =$

$(^-8)9 =$

$4(^-7) =$

$(^-6)4 =$

$(^-3)7 =$

$3(^-12) =$

$(^-8)10 =$

$6(^-9) =$

 0-88012-487-3

Signed Numbers

Find the Quotients

The quotient of two integers with like signs is a positive integer equal to the quotient of the integers.

$8 \div 4 = 2$
$(^-18) \div (^-9) = 2$

$54 \div 9 =$

$(^-12) \div (^-4) =$

The quotient of two integers with unlike signs is a negative integer equal to the quotient of the integers.

$(^-8) \div 4 = (^-2)$
$18 \div (^-9) = {}^-2$

study this first

$54 \div (^-9) =$

$(^-12) \div 4 =$

$\frac{56}{7} =$ $\frac{(^-56)}{(^-7)} =$ $\frac{(^-56)}{7} =$ $\frac{56}{(^-7)} =$

$\frac{14}{2} =$ $\frac{(^-14)}{(^-2)} =$ $\frac{(^-14)}{2} =$ $\frac{14}{(^-2)} =$

$\frac{21}{7} =$ $\frac{(^-21)}{(^-7)} =$ $\frac{(^-21)}{7} =$ $\frac{21}{(^-7)} =$

$\frac{45}{5} =$ $\frac{(^-45)}{(^-5)} =$ $\frac{(^-45)}{5} =$ $\frac{45}{(^-5)} =$

0-88012-487-3

Signed Numbers

Signed Numbers

Perform the operations indicated.

$7 \cdot 11 =$

$4 \cdot 9 =$

$(^{-}3)10 =$

$(^{-}6)12 =$

$2(^{-}9) =$

$2(^{-}12) =$

$(^{-}4)(^{-}15) =$

$(^{-}5)(^{-}10) =$

$20(^{-}4) =$

$5(^{-}13) =$

$6 \div 3 =$

$8 \div 2 =$

$16 \div (^{-}8) =$

$18 \div (^{-}3) =$

$(^{-}27) \div 9 =$

$(^{-}30) \div 6 =$

$(^{-}32) \div (^{-}8) =$

$(^{-}40) \div (^{-}5) =$

$56 \div (^{-}7) =$

$(^{-}54) \div 6 =$

0-88012-487-3

Signed Numbers

Signed Numbers

Perform the operations indicated.

$2 \cdot 7 =$	$3 \cdot 8 =$
$(^-3)11 =$	$(^-5)12 =$
$8(^-2) =$	$2(^-6) =$
$(^-4)5 =$	$(^-3)4 =$
$2 \cdot 18 =$	$4(^-12) =$
$10 \div 2 =$	$12 \div 6 =$
$22 \div (^-11) =$	$24 \div (^-2) =$
$(^-32) \div 4 =$	$(^-36) \div 3 =$
$(^-45) \div (^-9) =$	$(^-36) \div (^-2) =$
$80 \div (^-10) =$	$(^-63) \div (^-7) =$

0-88012-487-3

Signed Numbers

Combine the Terms

Combine the terms within each parenthesis. Then remove the parentheses and find the sums.

$(2-11) + (3-2) =$ $(^-9) + 1 = (^-8)$	$(3-1) + (2-5) =$ $2 + (^-3) = (^-1)$

$(3+5) + (4+9) =$ $\qquad$ $(3+10) + (2+9) =$

$(5+1) + (6+2) =$ $\qquad$ $(3+4) + (8+6) =$

$(8-4) + (7-2) =$ $\qquad$ $(6-1) + (4-3) =$

$(9-7) + (5-3) =$ $\qquad$ $(3-1) + (5-4) =$

$(1-6) + (8-12) =$ $\qquad$ $(3-7) + (5-15) =$

$(6-10) + (4-10) =$ $\qquad$ $(2-5) + (7-11) =$

0-88012-487-3

Signed Numbers

Combine the Terms

Combine the terms within each parenthesis. Then remove parentheses where possible and perform the operation indicated.

(3+2) – (2–1) = 5 – 1 = 4	(1–2) – (3–1) = (⁻1) – (2) = (⁻1) + (⁻2) = (⁻3)

(4+7) – (2+3) =

(3+5) – (6+1) =

(4+1) – (7+2) =

(3+5) – (9+4) =

(3–5) – (4+3) =

(6–9) – (6+2) =

(4+2) – (5–2) =

(2+6) – (3–1) =

(7+5) – (1–6) =

(9+6) – (8–12) =

(7–14) – (3–8) =

(4–9) – (1–13) =

0-88012-487-3

Signed Numbers

Combine the Terms

Combine the terms within each parenthesis. Then remove the parentheses where possible and find the product or the quotient.

How to start

$(-5)\ (3-5)\ =$

$({}^{-}5)\ ({}^{-}2)\ =\ 10$

$(17-9)\ \div\ (6-10)\ =$

$8\ \div\ ({}^{-}4)\ =\ {}^{-}2$

$({}^{-}3)(2+7)\ =$

$5(3-6)\ =$

$({}^{-}4)(6+2)\ =$

$({}^{-}7)(2-3)\ =$

$6(2-7)\ =$

$({}^{-}3)(7+2)\ =$

$(8+10)\ \div\ 6\ =$

$(30-10)\ \div\ 5\ =$

$(9+9)\ \div\ ({}^{-}2)\ =$

$(2-26)\ \div\ ({}^{-}8)\ =$

$(3-19)\ \div\ 8\ =$

$(27+15)\ \div\ ({}^{-}6)\ =$

0-88012-487-3

adding/subtracting/multiplying/dividing signed numbers

Signed Numbers

Combine the Terms

Combine the terms within each parenthesis. Then remove the parentheses where possible and perform the operation indicated.

$(12+7) + (9+7) =$ $\qquad$ $(6-3) + (2-8) =$

$(9+6) - (3+1) =$ $\qquad$ $(9-1) - (2-5) =$

$(1-12) + (4+8) =$ $\qquad$ $(2-13) + (6-8) =$

$(4-9) - (3+5) =$ $\qquad$ $(7-12) - (5-12) =$

$9(5+2) =$ $\qquad$ $(^{-}2)(7+8) =$

$(^{-}5)(3-6) =$ $\qquad$ $(12+15) \div (^{-}3) =$

$(7-29) \div 2 =$ $\qquad$ $(13-48) \div (^{-}5) =$

 0-88012-487-3

Signed Numbers

Combine the Terms

Combine the terms within each parenthesis. Then remove parentheses where possible and perform the operation indicated.

$(15+6) \;+\; (10+8) \;=$

$(5-4) \;+\; (7-9) \;=$

$(12+9) \;-\; (7-1) \;=$

$(12-3) \;-\; (5-8) \;=$

$(4-10) \;+\; (7-2) \;=$

$(3-16) \;+\; (1-5) \;=$

$(3-6) \;-\; (3+5) \;=$

$(2-9) \;-\; (8-16) \;=$

$6(8+2) \;=$

$(^{-}8)(5+2) \;=$

$(^{-}7)(5-9) \;=$

$(22+14) \;\div\; (^{-}12) \;=$

$(11-56) \;\div\; 9 \;=$

$(12-68) \;\div\; (^{-}7) \;=$

You have finished
Step 1

0-88012-487-3

Polynomials

Combine Like Terms

2a	3a	5b	6x
5a	6a	4b	7x
7a	2a	9b	5x
14a			

3ax	10cd	15b	8by
7ax	8cd	14b	9by
2ax	7cd	2b	6by

6b	15a	27ab	8x
−2b	− 3a	−14ab	−4x

7cd	12c	8d	32ab
− 3cd	− 7c	−5d	−16ab

4y	10y	5ay	15by
+ 7y	− 7y	+6ay	− 6by

0-88012-487-3

Polynomials

Combine Like Terms

$$\begin{array}{rcrcrcr} 3a & \quad & -6a & \quad & 15b & \quad & 20n \\ \underline{+4a} & & \underline{+4a} & & \underline{-7b} & & \underline{-9n} \\ 7a & & & & & & \end{array}$$

$$\begin{array}{rcrcrcr} 5a & \quad & 9cd & \quad & 11ab & \quad & 9x \\ 6a & & 14cd & & 12ab & & 7x \\ \underline{+9a} & & \underline{+8cd} & & \underline{+6ab} & & \underline{+5x} \end{array}$$

$$\begin{array}{rcrcrcr} 14b & \quad & -16a & \quad & -8x & \quad & 4y \\ -6b & & 12a & & -7x & & -9y \\ \underline{4b} & & \underline{-8a} & & \underline{12x} & & \underline{-3y} \end{array}$$

$$\begin{array}{rcrcrcr} 6a & \quad & 15b & \quad & 9ab & \quad & -16x \\ \underline{-12a} & & \underline{-8b} & & \underline{-17ab} & & \underline{8x} \end{array}$$

$$\begin{array}{rcrcrcr} 13ab & \quad & -8by & \quad & 4cd & \quad & 16b \\ \underline{-6ab} & & \underline{-10by} & & \underline{-12cd} & & \underline{-\ 7b} \end{array}$$

 0-88012-487-3

Polynomials

Combine Like Terms

Circle and combine like terms.

Here's an example

$2b^2 + 6b - 4a - 3b + c^2$

$6b - 3b = 3b$

$2^2 + 6ab + b^2 - 5ab + 3$

$5x^2 - b^2 + 3ax - 5ax + c^2$

$4b - 3c + 2b - 6a - 2 + 3b$

$3abx - 4bc + 3ab - bc$

$6 - 2cd - 3ad + 5ac + 6ad$

$4a^2 - 3abx + 6b^2 - 5abx + x^2$

0-88012-487-3

Polynomials

Combine Like Terms

Remove parentheses and combine like terms.

$4n + (6n - 8)$
$4n + 6n - 8$
$10n - 8$

$4n - (6n - 8)$

$8x + (2x - 5)$

$2n - (5n - 7)$

$(5x + 3y + z)$

$3a - (2b - 3c)$

$-(6a + b) + c$

$5y^2 + (4y - z)$

$2n - (8a + 2b)$

$(7x - y) + 3z$

$7x^2 - 3a - (4b)$

$-(ax - 3bx) + 4x$

0-88012-487-3

Polynomials

Add the Polynomials

$$\begin{array}{r} 14x^2 - 5x \\ + (12x^2 - 4x) \\ \hline 26x^2 - 9x \end{array}$$

$$\begin{array}{r} 7ax + 4a \\ + (-3ax - a) \\ \hline \end{array}$$

$$\begin{array}{r} -4x + 3y \\ + (-5x - 10y) \\ \hline \end{array}$$

$$\begin{array}{r} 25c - 6d \\ + (-15c + 5d) \\ \hline \end{array}$$

$$\begin{array}{r} -3b + 7 \\ + (-5b - 9) \\ \hline \end{array}$$

$$\begin{array}{r} x^2 - y \\ + (5x^2 + 3y) \\ \hline \end{array}$$

$$\begin{array}{r} 11ab + 4c \\ + (-12ab - 5c) \\ \hline \end{array}$$

$$\begin{array}{r} 9x - 5 \\ + (-4x + 10) \\ \hline \end{array}$$

$$\begin{array}{r} -7y - 4z \\ + (18y + 12z) \\ \hline \end{array}$$

Add $3x^2 - 5y$ and $-9x^2 + 4y$

Add $-a^2 - b$ and $5a^2 + 6b$

 0-88012-487-3

Polynomials

Add the Polynomials

$$\begin{array}{r} 2x^2 - x + 3 \\ + (5x^2 + 4x - 8) \\ \hline \end{array}$$

$$\begin{array}{r} 4a^2 - 3ab + b^2 \\ + (-9a^2 - ab - 5b^2) \\ \hline \end{array}$$

$$\begin{array}{r} 5x^4 - 3x^2 - 6 \\ + (-2x^4 + 7x^2 - 2) \\ \hline \end{array}$$

$$\begin{array}{r} 7x + 3y - 2z \\ + (-3x + 4y - 6z) \\ \hline \end{array}$$

$$\begin{array}{r} 4a^2 - 6b^2 + 7c^2 \\ + (-6a^2 + 4b^2 - 7c^2) \\ + (7a^2 + 3b^2 - 5c^2) \\ \hline \end{array}$$

$$\begin{array}{r} 10x^2 + x + 4 \\ + (9x^2 - 8x - 3) \\ + (-3x^2 + 2x - 5) \\ \hline \end{array}$$

$$\begin{array}{r} 8ab - 6ac - 4ad \\ + (-5ab + 4ac + 2ad) \\ + (-6ab - 7ac + 9ad) \\ \hline \end{array}$$

$$\begin{array}{r} 2a^2 + 6ab - 3b^2 \\ + (5a^2 + ab - 8b^2) \\ + (-9a^2 + 2ab + 5b^2) \\ \hline \end{array}$$

0-88012-487-3

Polynomials

Subtract the Polynomials

Example:

$$\begin{array}{r} 5x^2 - 7 \\ \underline{-\ (3x^2 - 2)} \\ 2x^2 - 5 \end{array}$$

$$\begin{array}{r} 12ab - 12c \\ \underline{-\ (3ab + 6c)} \end{array} \qquad \begin{array}{r} 7x + 5y \\ \underline{-\ (-\ 3x + 2y)} \end{array}$$

$$\begin{array}{r} 3b + c \\ \underline{-\ (-\ 4b - 2c)} \end{array} \qquad \begin{array}{r} 18x - 4 \\ \underline{-\ (14x + 3)} \end{array} \qquad \begin{array}{r} 2x^2 - 1 \\ \underline{-\ (-\ 3x^2 - 9)} \end{array}$$

$$\begin{array}{r} 4ax + 3b \\ \underline{-\ (-\ 5ax - 2b)} \end{array} \qquad \begin{array}{r} 4y^3 - 3y^2 \\ \underline{-\ (-\ 6y^3 - 5y^2)} \end{array} \qquad \begin{array}{r} -\ 2ay + 3y \\ \underline{-\ (-\ 6ay - 4y)} \end{array}$$

$$\begin{array}{r} -\ 3a - 4b \\ \underline{-\ (6a + 5b)} \end{array} \qquad \begin{array}{r} -\ 8b - 3 \\ \underline{-\ (-\ 10b - 4)} \end{array} \qquad \begin{array}{r} 4x^2 + 3x \\ \underline{-\ (5x^2 + 8x)} \end{array}$$

0-88012-487-3

Polynomials

Subtract the Polynomials

$16x^2 - 5$
$\underline{-(18x^2 + 4)}$

$3ab - 6c$
$\underline{-(4ab + 3c)}$

$-5y + 4$
$\underline{-(8y - 6)}$

$-6x - 4$
$\underline{-(-5x + 5)}$

$9ax + 8ay$
$\underline{-(4ax - 3ay)}$

$-7n + 3$
$\underline{-(-7n + 3)}$

$7y + 3z$
$\underline{-(-6y - 2z)}$

$15x^2 - 2x$
$\underline{-(-3x^2 - 5x)}$

$-4b - 3c$
$\underline{-(5b + 6c)}$

From $8x + 3y - 2z$ subtract $-2x - 2y + z$

Subtract $-3x^2 + 5x - 2$ from $4x^2 - 6x - 4$

0-88012-487-3

Polynomials

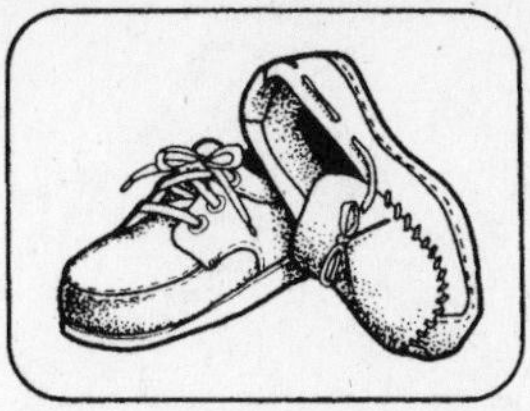

Subtract the Polynomials

$$\begin{array}{r} -3xy-5 \\ \underline{-(-8xy+2)} \end{array} \qquad \begin{array}{r} 7y+3z \\ \underline{-(-4y+3z)} \end{array} \qquad \begin{array}{r} -2x^2+5 \\ \underline{-(3x^2-4)} \end{array}$$

$$\begin{array}{r} 5ab+2z \\ \underline{-(3ab+z)} \end{array} \qquad \begin{array}{r} -6x-5 \\ \underline{-(-4x+2)} \end{array} \qquad \begin{array}{r} 4y+10 \\ \underline{-(-y+8)} \end{array}$$

$$\begin{array}{r} x+y \\ \underline{-(-3x-5y)} \end{array} \qquad \begin{array}{r} 2b+3c \\ \underline{-(-3b+6c)} \end{array} \qquad \begin{array}{r} 8x-2y \\ \underline{-(5x+2y)} \end{array}$$

Subtract $5x^2-8x-10$ from $-6x^2-3x-8$

From $3a+7b+6c$ subtract $-8a-2b-2c$

0-88012-487-3

Polynomials

Combine Like Terms

Remove parentheses and brackets and combine like terms.

$5x + [(3x - 4) + 6]$
$5x + 3x - 4 + 6$
$8x + 2$

$5x - [6-(3x-4)]$

$4a + [3a + (a-z)]$

$6b - [5+(4b-8)]$

$(3x-5) - (5x-3)$

$[(4a-b)+b] - 5a$

$x^2 + (3x^2-5x+3)$

$4ab - (-3ab+3a+6)$

$5a + [4-(-6a+2)]$

$3x - [(-4x+3)+6x]$

0-88012-487-3

Polynomials

Combine Like Terms

Remove parentheses and brackets and combine like terms.

$3a + [8 - (4a + 7)]$
$3a + [8 - 4a - 7]$
$3a + 8 - 4a - 7$
$-a + 1$

$4x - [3 - (-5x + 7)]$

$2x + [5 + (-4x - 6)]$

$3a - [8 - (4a - 7)]$

$-(5b - 6) - (-2b + 4)$

$7y - (3y^2 - 4y - 4)$

$[6x - (4x - 2)] + 3$

$[4ab + (6ab - 2)] - 3ab$

$-(4x - 3y) - (6x + 8y)$

$6b - [5 - (6b - 5)]$

0-88012-487-3

Polynomials

Combine Like Terms

Remove parentheses and brackets and combine like terms.

$$[(8x+3) - (5x-8) - (7x+1)]$$

$$-\ [-(6x+5) + (4x-3)]$$

$$-\ [(3x-4y-2z) - (8x-6y+3z)]$$

$$[-(6x+4) - (3x-5y)]\ - (4x+3y)$$

 0-88012-487-3

Polynomials

Find the Products

$3(x+y)$ $3x+3y$	$a(x-2)$	$x(x-y)$
$5(x-y)$	$3(a+b)$	$a(b+5)$
$4x(a-b)$	$y(5-a)$	$6(3b-c)$
$3a(a+b)$	$5x(x+y)$	$3(4x-3y)$
$5(2a-4b)$	$2a(x+y)$	$4ab(x-y)$
$6x(-x+y)$	$5(-2-a)$	$-2(x+2y)$

 0-88012-487-3

Polynomials

Find the Products

$5(a+b)$ $5a+5b$	$x(3y+z)$	$n(3n+4)$
$6a(-x+y)$	$b(a-c)$	$x(5x-2y)$
$3b(4b+5)$	$-4(ab+cd)$	$a(3x+4y)$
$x^2(a+b)$	$-2n^2(n-1)$	$5y(y-3)$
$5y(6+y)$	$-x(x+3xy)$	$5a(-b+c)$
$x^2(-x-y)$	$\frac{1}{2}(2x+6y)$	$3x^2(2x-2y)$

0-88012-487-3

Polynomials

Collect Like Terms

Simplify and collect like terms.

$$2(x-y) - 3(x+y) + 5(2x-y)$$
$$2x-2y-3x-3y+10x-5y$$
$$9x-10y$$

We did this one for you

$$4(2a+3b) + 2(a-4b) - 5(3a-b)$$

$$3x(2x+3) + x(-4x-5) - 6x$$

$$4[2(x+2y) + 3x] \quad -6(3x-2y)$$

$$3a(2a-6) - (5a+8) + 2(3a^2+4a)$$

0-88012-487-3

Polynomials

Collect Like Terms

Simplify and collect like terms.

$$-3\,[2x(x+3) - 2(x^2+3x)] - 5x(2x+3)$$

$$a(4a+3b+6) - 2a(-3a-5b-2)$$

$$3x(2x+5) - x(-4x-2) + 5(2x^2+3x+1)$$

$$4x(a-3b) - 2\,[x(2a-b) - (4ax+2bx)]$$

You have finished
Step
2

 0-88012-487-3

Equations

Write the Equations

Let n stand for the unknown.

Four times what number equals sixteen?

What number plus seven equals fifteen?

A number divided by six minus four equals twelve.

A number minus sixteen equals two.

Three times what number plus seven equals thirteen?

A number divided in half plus fourteen equals twenty.

 0-88012-487-3

Equations

Write the Equations

Let n equal the unknown.

Twice a number minus six equals the number plus seven.

The product of five and a number equals one-half the number plus eighteen.

Four-fifths of what number plus sixteen equals twenty-four.

A number plus fifteen is equal to twice the number minus eight.

Two times the sum of a number and six equals eighteen.

Four times a number minus one-half the number equals twenty-one.

0-88012-487-3

Equations

Write the Equations

Let n equal the unknown.

Eighteen minus the product of four and a number equals ten.

Twenty-six is equal to a number divided by five plus seven.

Three times a number plus six times that same number equals twenty-four.

Four times the sum of a number plus six equals thirty.

A number minus four and one-third equals eight.

Seven times a number divided by three minus six equals three times the number.

 0-88012-487-3

Equations

Check the Equations

Here's how

Check $3 + n = 7$ for:

$n = 4$ (circled)	$n = 6$
$3 + n = 7$	$3 + n = 7$
$3 + (4) = 7$	$3 + (6) = 7$
$7 = 7$	$9 \neq 7$

Check $6 + n = 8$ for:

$n = 6$ $\qquad$ $n = 2$

Check $n + 5 = 14$ for:

$n = 8$ $\qquad$ $n = 9$

Check $n - 8 = 2$ for:

$n = 12$ $\qquad$ $n = 10$

 0-88012-487-3

Equations

Check the Equations

Check $4n + 3n = 21$ for:

$n = 3$ (circled)	$n = 5$
$4n + 3n = 21$	$4n + 3n = 21$
$4(3) + 3(3) = 21$	$4(5) + 3(5) = 21$
$12 + 9 = 21$	$20 + 15 = 21$
$21 = 21$	$35 \neq 21$

Check $3n + 5n = 16$ for:

$n = 3$ $\qquad$ $n = 2$

Check $5n + n = 18$ for:

$n = 2$ $\qquad$ $n = 3$

Check $3n + 7n = 30$ for:

$n = 3$ $\qquad$ $n = 10$

0-88012-487-3

Number Table

Complete the table.
Using the values given for x, y or the solutions, find the missing numbers.

x (across the top); y (down the left side)

$2x + y =$	7		1		3
2		18	4		
6				6	
5	19			5	
		25			15
4			6		10

0-88012-487-3

TUTOR'S GUIDE
Mathematics Level 8

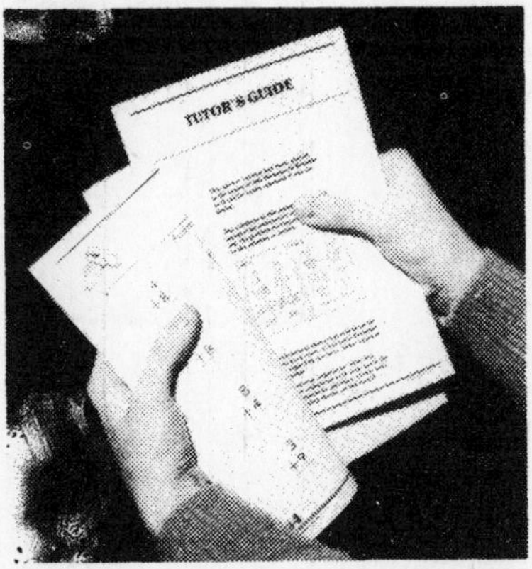

This answer section has been placed in the center of this Homework Booklet so it can be easily removed if you so desire.

The solutions in this manual reflect the layout of the exercises to simplify checking. The problem solving process as well as the solution is shown.

page 1	
2 + 6 = **8**	(2) + (6) = **(-8)**
9 + 7 = **16**	(9) + (7) = **(-16)**
6 + 1 = **7**	(6) + (1) = **(-7)**
11 + 6 = **17**	(11) + (6) = **(-17)**
6 + 3 = **9**	(6) + (3) = **(-9)**
7 + 6 + 8 + 2 = **23**	
(7) + (6) + (8) + (2) = **(-23)**	
6 + 1 + 9 + 7 = **22**	
(6) + (1) + (9) + (7) = **(-22)**	

page 2	
5 + (-4) = **1**	(5) + 4 = **(-1)**
8 + (5) = **3**	(8) + 5 = **(-3)**
(7) + 10 = **3**	7 + (10) = **(-3)**
(11) + 3 = **(-8)**	11 + (3) = **8**
3 + (7) = **(-4)**	(3) + 7 = **4**
(12) + 10 = **(-2)**	12 + (10) = **2**
7 + (12) = **(-5)**	(7) + 12 = **5**
(8) + 15 = **7**	8 + (15) = **(-7)**
4 + (2) = **2**	(4) + 2 = **(-2)**

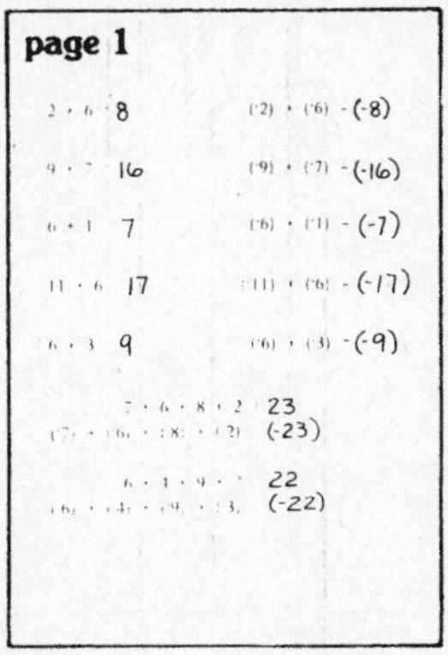

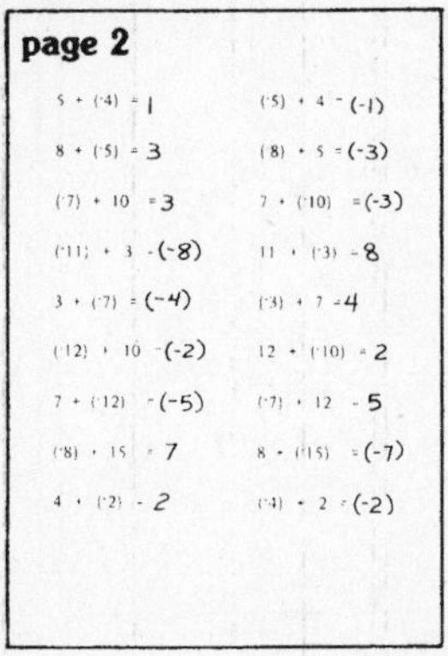

A motivational award is provided on the inside back cover. It has been designed to be signed by the tutor, either a parent or teacher.

Motivational suggestion: After the student completes each step, mark the achievement by placing a sticker next to that step shown on the award.

0-88012-487-3

Solutions

page 3

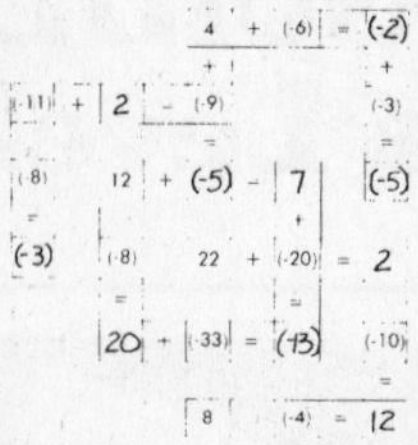

4 + (-6) = (-2)
(-11) + 2 - (-9)
(-3)
(-8) 12 + (-5) - 7 (-5)
(-3) (-8) 22 + (-20) = 2
20 + (-33) = (-13) (-10)
8 (-4) = 12

page 4

5 + (-3) + 2 + (-1) = 7 + (-4) = 3
(-2) + 4 + 3 + (-3) = (-5) + 7 = 2
3 + 2 + (-2) + (-3) = 5 + (-5) = 0
6 + (-2) + (-1) + (-3) = 6 + (-6) = 0
(-3) + (-1) + 2 + 1 = (-4) + 3 = (-1)
4 + 7 + (-1) + (-3) = 11 + (-4) = 7
6 + 3 + 1 + (-2) = 10 + (-2) = 8
3 + (-3) + (-3) + (-2) = 3 + (-8) = (-5)

page 5

2 + (-1) + 4 + (-3) = 6 + (-4) = 2
(-1) + (-5) + 2 + 3 = (-6) + 5 = (-1)
4 + (-2) + (-2) + (-3) = 4 + (-7) = (-3)
(-6) + 3 + (-2) + 6 = (-8) + 9 = 1
(-5) + 2 + (-5) + 1 = (-10) + 3 = (-7)
6 + 2 + (-3) + 3 = 11 + (-3) = 8
7 + (-3) + (-4) + 1 = 8 + (-7) = 1
1 + (-3) + (-3) + 1 = 2 + (-6) = (-4)

page 6

3 − (-8) = 3 + 8 = 11
(-3) − (-8) = (-3) + 8 = 5
(-3) − 8 = (-3) + (-8) = (-11)
3 − 8 = 3 + (-8) = (-5)
(-7) − (-6) = (-7) + 6 = (-1)
(-7) − 6 = (-7) + (-6) = (-13)
7 − (-6) = 7 + 6 = 13
7 − 6 = 7 + (-6) = 1

page 7

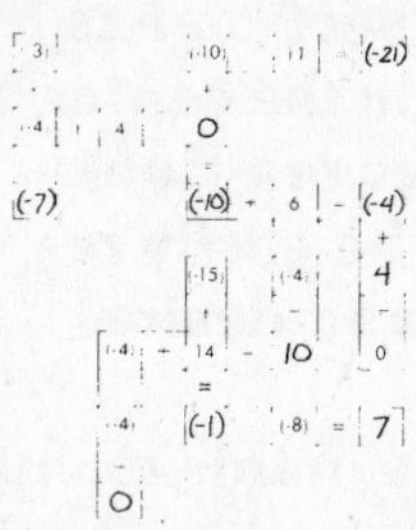

3 (-10) 11 (-21)
-4 4 0
(-7) (-10) + 6 - (-4)
(-15) (-4) 4
(-4) + 14 - 10 0
(-4) (-1) (-8) = 7
0

page 8

4 − (-10) = 4 + 10 = 14
(-4) − 10 = (-4) + (-10) = (-14)
(-4) − (-10) = (-4) + 10 = 6
4 − 10 = 4 + (-10) = (-6)
(-15) − 8 = (-15) + (-8) = (-23)
(-15) − (-8) = (-15) + 8 = (-7)
15 − 8 = 15 + (-8) = 7
15 − (-8) = 15 + 8 = 23

page 9

			-6
-4	6	-8	-6
-6	-2	2	-6
4	-10	0	-6
-6	-6	-6	-6

page 10

5 + 9 = 14
(-5) + (-11) = (-16)
(-12) + (-6) = (-18)
3 + (-8) = (-5)
4 + (-7) = (-3)
12 + (-7) = 5
(-9) + 10 = 1
10 + (-4) = 6
8 + (-10) = (-2)
(-10) − (-14) = (-10) + 14 = 4
(-12) − (-8) = (-12) + 8 = (-4)
(-13) − (-10) = (-13) + 10 = -3
12 − (-6) = 12 + 6 = 18
6 − (-15) = 6 + 15 = 21
9 + (-12) + 15 + (-16) = 24 + (-28) = (-4)

page 11

			3
-1	9	-5	3
3	1	5	3
7	-7	3	3
3	3	3	3

page 12

3 · 4 = 12
3(-4) = (-12)
(-8)(-9) = 72
(-8)9 = (-72)
(-4)(-7) = 28
4(-7) = (-28)
6 · 4 = 24
(-6)4 = (-24)
3 · 7 = 21
(-3)7 = (-21)
(-3)(-12) = 36
3(-12) = (-36)
8 · 10 = 80
(-8)10 = (-80)
(-6)(-9) = 54
6(-9) = (-54)

page 13

54 ÷ 9 = 6
54 ÷ (-9) = (-6)
(-12) ÷ (-4) = 3
(-12) ÷ 4 = (-3)
$\frac{56}{7} = 8$ $\frac{(-56)}{(-7)} = 8$ $\frac{(-56)}{7} = (-8)$ $\frac{56}{(-7)} = (-8)$
$\frac{14}{2} = 7$ $\frac{(-14)}{(-2)} = 7$ $\frac{(-14)}{2} = (-7)$ $\frac{14}{(-2)} = (-7)$
$\frac{21}{7} = 3$ $\frac{(-21)}{(-7)} = 3$ $\frac{(-21)}{7} = (-3)$ $\frac{21}{(-7)} = (-3)$
$\frac{45}{5} = 9$ $\frac{(-45)}{(-5)} = 9$ $\frac{(-45)}{5} = (-9)$ $\frac{45}{(-5)} = (-9)$

page 14

7 · 11 = 77
4 · 9 = 36
(-3)10 = (-30)
(-6)12 = (-72)
2(-9) = (-18)
2(-12) = (-24)
(-4)(-15) = 60
(-5)(-10) = 50
20(-4) = (-80)
5(-13) = (-65)
6 ÷ 3 = 2
8 ÷ 2 = 4
16 ÷ (-8) = (-2)
18 ÷ (-3) = (-6)
(-27) ÷ 9 = (-3)
(-30) ÷ 6 = (-5)
(-32) ÷ (-8) = 4
(-40) ÷ (-5) = 8
56 ÷ (-7) = (-8)
(-54) ÷ 6 = (-9)

0-88012-487-3

page 15

$2 \cdot 7 = 14$ | $3 \cdot 8 = 24$

$(-3)11 = (-33)$ | $(-5)12 = (-60)$

$8(-2) = (-16)$ | $2(-6) = (-12)$

$(-4)5 = (-20)$ | $(-3)4 = (-12)$

$2 \cdot 18 = 36$ | $4(-12) = (-48)$

$10 \div 2 = 5$ | $12 \div 6 = 2$

$22 \div (-11) = (-2)$ | $24 \div (-2) = (-12)$

$(-32) \div 4 = (-8)$ | $(-36) \div 3 = (-12)$

$(-45) \div (-9) = 5$ | $(-36) \div (-2) = 18$

$80 \div (-10) = (-8)$ | $(-63) \div (-7) = 9$

page 16

$(3+5) + (4+9) = 8 + 13 = 21$ | $(3+10) + (2+9) = 13 + 11 = 24$

$(5+1) + (6+2) = 6 + 8 = 14$ | $(3+4) + (8+6) = 7 + 14 = 21$

$(8-4) + (7-2) = 4 + 5 = 9$ | $(6-1) + (4-3) = 5 + 1 = 6$

$(9-7) + (5-3) = 2 + 2 = 4$ | $(3-1) + (5-4) = 2 + 1 = 3$

$(1-6) + (8-12) = (-5) + (-4) = (-9)$ | $(3-7) + (5-15) = (-4) + (-10) = (-14)$

$(6-10) + (4-10) = (-4) + (-6) = (-10)$ | $(2-5) + (7-11) = (-3) + (-4) = (-7)$

page 17

$(4+7) - (2+3) = 11 - 5 = 11 + (-5) = 6$ | $(3+5) - (6+1) = 8 - 7 = 8 + (-7) = 1$

$(4+1) - (7+2) = 5 - 9 = 5 + (-9) = (-4)$ | $(3+5) - (9+4) = 8 - 13 = 8 + (-13) = (-5)$

$(3-5) - (4+3) = (-2) - 7 = (-2) + (-7) = (-9)$ | $(6-9) - (6+2) = (-3) - 8 = (-3) + (-8) = (-11)$

$(4+2) - (5-2) = 6 - 3 = 6 + (-3) = 3$ | $(2+6) - (3-1) = 8 - 2 = 8 + (-2) = 6$

$(7+5) - (1-6) = 12 - (-5) = 12 + 5 = 17$ | $(9+6) - (8-12) = 15 - (-4) = 15 + 4 = 19$

$(7-14) - (3-8) = (-7) - (-5) = (-7) + 5 = (-2)$ | $(4-9) - (1-13) = (-5) - (-12) = (-5) + 12 = 7$

page 18

$(-3)(2+7) = (-3) \cdot 9 = (-27)$ | $5(3-6) = 5(-3) = (-15)$

$(-4)(6+2) = (-4) \cdot 8 = (-32)$ | $(-7)(2-3) = (-7) \cdot (-1) = 7$

$6(2-7) = 6(-5) = (-30)$ | $(-3)(7+2) = (-3) \cdot 9 = (-27)$

$(8+10) \div 6 = 18 \div 6 = 3$ | $(30-10) \div 5 = 20 \div 5 = 4$

$(9+9) \div (-2) = 18 \div (-2) = (-9)$ | $(2-26) \div (-8) = (-24) \div (-8) = 3$

$(3-19) \div 8 = (-16) \div 8 = (-2)$ | $(27+15) \div (-6) = 42 \div (-6) = (-7)$

page 19

$(12+7) + (9+7) = 19 + 16 = 35$ | $(6-3) + (2-8) = 3 + (-6) = (-3)$

$(9+6) - (3+1) = 15 - 4 = 15 + (-4) = 11$ | $(9-1) - (2-5) = 8 - (-3) = 8 + 3 = 11$

$(1-12) + (4+8) = (-11) + 12 = 1$ | $(2-13) + (6-8) = (-11) + (-2) = (-13)$

$(4-9) - (3+5) = (-5) - 8 = (-5) + (-8) = (-13)$ | $(7-12) - (5-12) = (-5) - (-7) = (-5) + 7 = 2$

$9(5+2) = 9 \cdot 7 = 63$ | $(-2)(7+8) = (-2) \cdot 15 = (-30)$

$(-5)(3-6) = (-5)(-3) = 15$ | $(12+15) \div (-3) = 27 \div (-3) = (-9)$

$(7-29) \div 2 = (-22) \div 2 = (-11)$ | $(13-48) \div (-5) = (-35) \div (-5) = 7$

page 20

$(15+6) + (10+8) = 21 + 18 = 39$ | $(5-4) + (7-9) = 1 + (-2) = (-1)$

$(12+9) - (7-1) = 21 - 6 = 21 + (-6) = 15$ | $(12-3) - (5-8) = 9 - (-3) = 9 + 3 = 12$

$(4-10) + (7-2) = (-6) + 5 = (-1)$ | $(3-16) + (1-5) = (-13) + (-4) = (-17)$

$(3-6) - (3+5) = (-3) - 8 = (-3) + (-8) = (-11)$ | $(2-9) - (8-16) = (-7) - (-8) = (-7) + 8 = 1$

$6(8+2) = 6 \cdot 10 = 60$ | $(-8)(5+2) = (-8) \cdot 7 = (-56)$

$(-7)(5-9) = (-7)(-4) = 28$ | $(22+14) \div (-12) = 36 \div (-12) = (-3)$

$(11-56) \div 9 = (-45) \div 9 = (-5)$ | $(12-68) \div (-7) = (-56) \div (-7) = 8$

page 21

$3a + 6a + 2a = 11a$ | $5b + 4b + 9b = 18b$ | $6x + 7x + 5x = 18x$

$3ax + 7ax + 2ax = 12ax$ | $10cd + 8cd + 7cd = 25cd$ | $15b + 14b + 2b = 31b$ | $8by + 9by + 6by = 23by$

$6b - 2b = 4b$ | $15a - 3a = 12a$ | $27ab - 14ab = 13ab$ | $8x - 4x = 4x$

$7cd - 3cd = 4cd$ | $12c - 7c = 5c$ | $8d - 5d = 3d$ | $32ab - 16ab = 16ab$

$4y + 7y = 11y$ | $10y - 7y = 3y$ | $5ay + 6ay = 11ay$ | $15by - 6by = 9by$

page 22

$-6a + 4a = -2a$ | $15b - 7b = 8b$ | $20n - 9n = 11n$

$5a + 6a + 9a = 20a$ | $9cd + 14cd + 8cd = 31cd$ | $11ab + 12ab + 6ab = 29ab$ | $9x + 7x + 5x = 21x$

$14b - 6b + 4b = 12b$ | $-16a + 12a - 8a = -12a$ | $-8x - 7x + 12x = -3x$ | $4y - 9y - 3y = -8y$

$6a - 12a = -6a$ | $15b - 8b = 7b$ | $9ab - 17ab = -8ab$ | $-16x + 8x = -8x$

$13ab - 6ab = 7ab$ | $-8by - 10by = -18by$ | $4cd - 12cd = -8cd$ | $16b - 7b = 9b$

page 23

$a^2 + 6ab + b^2 - 5ab + 3$
$+6ab - 5ab = 1ab$

$5x^2 - b^2 + 3ax - 5ax + c^2$
$+3ax - 5ax = -2ax$

$4b - 3c + 2b - 6a - 2 + 3b$
$+4b + 2b + 3b = 9b$

$3abx - 4bc + 3ab - bc$
$-4bc - bc = -5bc$

$6 - 2cd - 3ad + 5ac + 6ad$
$-3ad + 6ad = 3ad$

$4a^2 - 3abx + 6b^2 - 5abx + x^2$
$-3abx - 5abx = -8abx$

page 24

$4n - (6n - 8) = 4n - 6n + 8 = -2n + 8$

$8x + (2x - 5) = 8x + 2x - 5 = 10x - 5$ | $2n - (5n - 7) = 2n - 5n + 7 = -3n + 7$

$(5x + 3y + z) = 5x + 3y + z$ | $3a - (2b - 3c) = 3a - 2b + 3c$

$-(6a + b) + c = -6a - b + c$ | $5y^2 + (4y - z) = 5y^2 + 4y - z$

$2n - (8a + 2b) = 2n - 8a - 2b$ | $(7x - y) + 3z = 7x - y + 3z$

$7x^2 - 3a - (4b) = 7x^2 - 3a - 4b$ | $-(ax - 3bx) + 4x = -ax + 3bx + 4x$

page 25

$7ax + 4a + (-3ax - a) = 4ax + 3a$ | $-4x + 3y + (-5x - 10y) = -9x - 7y$

$25c - 6d + (-15c + 5d) = 10c - d$ | $-3b + 7 + (-5b - 9) = -8b - 2$ | $x^2 - y + (5x^2 + 3y) = 6x^2 + 2y$

$11ab + 4c + (-12ab - 5c) = -ab - c$ | $9x - 5 + (-4x + 10) = 5x + 5$ | $-7y - 4z + (18y + 12z) = 11y + 8z$

Add $3x^2 - 5y$ and $-9x^2 + 4y$: $3x^2 - 5y + (-9x^2 + 4y) = -6x^2 - y$

Add $-a^2 - b$ and $5a^2 + 6b$: $-a^2 - b + 5a^2 + 6b = 4a^2 + 5b$

page 26

$2x^2 - x + 3 + (5x^2 + 4x - 8) = 7x^2 + 3x - 5$ | $4a^2 - 3ab + b^2 + (-9a^2 - ab - 5b^2) = -5a^2 - 4ab - 4b^2$

$5x^4 - 3x^2 - 6 + (-2x^4 + 7x^2 - 2) = 3x^4 + 4x^2 - 8$ | $7x + 3y - 2z + (-3x + 4y - 6z) = 4x + 7y - 8z$

$4a^2 - 6b^2 + 7c^2 + (-6a^2 + 4b^2 - 7c^2) + (7a^2 + 3b^2 - 5c^2) = 5a^2 + b^2 - 5c^2$ | $10x^2 + x + 4 + (9x^2 - 8x - 3) + (-3x^2 + 2x - 5) = 16x^2 - 5x - 4$

$8ab - 6ac - 4ad + (-5ab + 4ac + 2ad) + (-6ab - 7ac + 9ad) = -3ab - 9ac + 7ad$ | $2a^2 + 6ab - 3b^2 + (5a^2 + ab - 8b^2) + (-9a^2 + 2ab + 5b^2) = -2a^2 + 9ab - 6b^2$

Solutions

0-88012-487-3

Solutions

page 27

- $12ab - 12c$; $-(3ab + 6c)$; $9ab - 18c$
- $7x + 5y$; $-(-3x + 2y)$; $10x + 3y$
- $3b + c$; $-(-4b - 2c)$; $7b + 3c$
- $18x - 4$; $-(14x + 3)$; $4x - 7$
- $2x^2 - 1$; $-(-3x^2 - 9)$; $5x^2 + 8$
- $4ax + 3b$; $-(-5ax - 2b)$; $9ax + 5b$
- $4y^3 - 3y^2$; $-(-6y^3 - 5y^2)$; $10y^3 + 2y^2$
- $-2ay + 3y$; $-(-6ay - 4y)$; $4ay + 7y$
- $-3a - 4b$; $-(6a + 5b)$; $-9a - 9b$
- $-8b - 3$; $-(-10b - 4)$; $2b + 1$
- $4x^2 + 3x$; $-(5x^2 + 8x)$; $-x^2 - 5x$

page 28

- $16x^2 - 5$; $-(18x^2 + 4)$; $-2x^2 - 9$
- $3ab - 6c$; $-(4ab + 3c)$; $-ab - 9c$
- $-5y + 4$; $-(8y - 6)$; $-13y + 10$
- $-6x - 4$; $-(-5x + 5)$; $-x - 9$
- $9ax + 8ay$; $-(4ax - 3ay)$; $5ax + 11ay$
- $-7n + 3$; $-(-7n + 3)$; 0
- $7y + 3z$; $-(-6y - 2z)$; $13y + 5z$
- $15x^2 - 2x$; $-(-3x^2 - 5x)$; $18x^2 + 3x$
- $-4b - 3c$; $-(5b + 6c)$; $-9b - 9c$

From $8x + 3y - 2z$ subtract $-2x - 2y + z$

$8x + 3y - 2z$; $-(-2x - 2y + z)$; $10x + 5y - 3z$

Subtract $-3x^2 + 5x - 2$ from $4x^2 - 6x - 4$

$4x^2 - 6x - 4$; $-(-3x^2 + 5x - 2)$; $7x^2 - 11x - 2$

page 29

- $-3xy - 5$; $-(-8xy + 2)$; $5xy - 7$
- $7y + 3z$; $-(-4y + 3z)$; $11y$
- $-2x^2 + 5$; $-(3x^2 - 4)$; $-5x^2 + 9$
- $5ab + 2z$; $-(3ab + z)$; $2ab + z$
- $-6x - 5$; $-(-4x + 2)$; $-2x - 7$
- $4y + 10$; $-(-y + 8)$; $5y + 2$
- $x + y$; $-(-3x - 5y)$; $4x + 6y$
- $2b + 3c$; $-(-3b + 6c)$; $5b - 3c$
- $8x - 2y$; $-(5x + 2y)$; $3x - 4y$

Subtract $5x^2 - 8x - 10$ from $-6x^2 - 3x - 8$

$-6x^2 - 3x - 8$; $-(5x^2 - 8x - 10)$; $-11x^2 + 5x + 2$

From $3a + 7b + 6c$ subtract $-8a - 2b - 2c$

$3a + 7b + 6c$; $-(-8a - 2b - 2c)$; $11a + 9b + 8c$

page 30

- $5x - [6 - (3x - 4)]$; $5x - [6 - 3x + 4]$; $5x - 6 + 3x - 4$; $8x - 10$
- $4a + [3a + (a - z)]$; $4a + [3a + a - z]$; $4a + 3a + a - z$; $8a - z$
- $6b - [5 + (4b - 8)]$; $6b - [5 + 4b - 8]$; $6b - 5 - 4b + 8$; $2b + 3$
- $(3x - 5) - (5x - 3)$; $3x - 5 - 5x + 3$; $-2x - 2$
- $[(4a - b) + b] - 5a$; $[4a - b + b] - 5a$; $4a - b + b - 5a$; $-a$
- $x^2 + (3x^2 - 5x + 3)$; $x^2 + 3x^2 - 5x + 3$; $4x^2 - 5x + 3$
- $4ab - (-3ab + 3a + 6)$; $4ab + 3ab - 3a - 6$; $7ab - 3a - 6$
- $5a + [4 - (-6a + 2)]$; $5a + [4 + 6a - 2]$; $5a + 4 + 6a - 2$; $11a + 2$
- $3x - [(-4x + 3) + 6x]$; $3x - [-4x + 3 + 6x]$; $3x + 4x - 3 - 6x$; $x - 3$

page 31

- $4x - [3 - (-5x + 7)]$; $4x - [3 + 5x - 7]$; $4x - 3 - 5x + 7$; $-x + 4$
- $2x + [5 + (-4x - 6)]$; $2x + [5 - 4x - 6]$; $2x + 5 - 4x - 6$; $-2x - 1$
- $3a - [8 - (4a - 7)]$; $3a - [8 - 4a + 7]$; $3a - 8 + 4a - 7$; $7a - 15$
- $-(5b - 6) - (-2b + 4)$; $-5b + 6 + 2b - 4$; $-3b + 2$
- $7y - (3y^2 - 4y - 4)$; $7y - 3y^2 + 4y + 4$; $-3y^2 + 11y + 4$
- $[6x - (4x - 2)] + 3$; $[6x - 4x + 2] + 3$; $6x - 4x + 2 + 3$; $2x + 5$
- $[4ab + (6ab - 2)] - 3ab$; $[4ab + 6ab - 2] - 3ab$; $4ab + 6ab - 2 - 3ab$; $7ab - 2$
- $-(4x - 3y) - (6x + 8y)$; $-4x + 3y - 6x - 8y$; $-10x - 5y$
- $6b - [5 - (6b - 5)]$; $6b - [5 - 6b + 5]$; $6b - 5 + 6b - 5$; $12b - 10$

page 32

- $[(8x + 3) - (5x - 8) - (7x + 1)]$; $[8x + 3 - 5x + 8 - 7x - 1]$; $8x + 3 - 5x + 8 - 7x - 1$; $-4x + 10$
- $-[-(6x + 5) + (4x - 3)]$; $-[-6x - 5 + 4x - 3]$; $+6x + 5 - 4x + 3$; $2x + 8$
- $-[(3x - 4y - 2z) - (8x - 6y + 3z)]$; $-[3x - 4y - 2z - 8x + 6y - 3z]$; $-3x + 4y + 2z + 8x - 6y + 3z$; $5x - 2y + 5z$
- $[-(6x + 4) - (3x - 5y)] - (4x + 3y)$; $[-6x - 4 - 3x + 5y] - 4x - 3y$; $-6x - 4 - 3x + 5y - 4x - 3y$; $-13x + 2y - 4$

page 33

- $a(x - 2)$; $ax - 2a$
- $x(x - y)$; $x^2 - xy$
- $5(x - y)$; $5x - 5y$
- $3(a + b)$; $3a + 3b$
- $a(b + 5)$; $ab + 5a$
- $4x(a - b)$; $4ax - 4bx$
- $y(5 - a)$; $5y - ay$
- $6(3b - c)$; $18b - 6c$
- $3a(a + b)$; $3a^2 + 3ab$
- $5x(x + y)$; $5x^2 + 5xy$
- $3(4x - 3y)$; $12x - 9y$
- $5(2a - 4b)$; $10a - 20b$
- $2a(x + y)$; $2ax + 2ay$
- $4ab(x - y)$; $4abx - 4aby$
- $6x(-x + y)$; $-6x^2 + 6xy$
- $5(-2 - a)$; $-10 - 5a$
- $-2(x + 2y)$; $-2x - 4y$

page 34

- $x(3y + z)$; $3xy + xz$
- $n(3n + 4)$; $3n^2 + 4n$
- $6a(-x + y)$; $-6ax + 6ay$
- $b(a - c)$; $ab - bc$
- $x(5x - 2y)$; $5x^2 - 2xy$
- $3b(4b + 5)$; $12b^2 + 15b$
- $-4(ab + cd)$; $-4ab - 4cd$
- $a(3x + 4y)$; $3ax + 4ay$
- $x^2(a + b)$; $ax^2 + bx^2$
- $-2n^2(n - 1)$; $-2n^3 + 2n^2$
- $5y(y - 3)$; $5y^2 - 15y$
- $5y(6 + y)$; $30y + 5y^2$
- $-x(x + 3xy)$; $-x^2 - 3x^2y$
- $5a(-b + c)$; $-5ab + 5ac$
- $x^2(-x - y)$; $-x^3 - x^2y$
- $\frac{1}{2}(2x + 6y)$; $x + 3y$
- $3x^2(2x - 2y)$; $6x^3 - 6x^2y$

page 35

- $4(2a + 3b) + 2(a - 4b) - 5(3a - b)$; $8a + 12b + 2a - 8b - 15a + 5b$; $-5a + 9b$
- $3x(2x + 3) + x(-4x - 5) - 6x$; $6x^2 + 9x - 4x^2 - 5x - 6x$; $2x^2 - 2x$
- $4[2(x + 2y) + 3x] - 6(3x - 2y)$; $4[2x + 4y + 3x] - 18x + 12y$; $8x + 16y + 12x - 18x + 12y$; $2x + 28y$
- $3a(2a - 6) - (5a + 8) + 2(3a^2 + 4a)$; $6a^2 - 18a - 5a - 8 + 6a^2 + 8a$; $12a^2 - 15a - 8$

page 36

- $-3[2x(x + 3) - 2(x^2 + 3x)] - 5x(2x + 3)$; $-3[2x^2 + 6x - 2x^2 - 6x] - 10x^2 - 15x$; $-6x^2 - 18x + 6x^2 + 18x - 10x^2 - 15x$; $-10x^2 - 15x$
- $a(4a + 3b + 6) - 2a(-3a - 5b - 2)$; $4a^2 + 3ab + 6a + 6a^2 + 10ab + 4a$; $10a^2 + 10a + 13ab$
- $3x(2x + 5) - x(-4x - 2) + 5(2x^2 + 3x + 1)$; $6x^2 + 15x + 4x^2 + 2x + 10x^2 + 15x + 5$; $20x^2 + 32x + 5$
- $4x(a - 3b) - 2[x(2a - b) - (4ax + 2bx)]$; $4ax - 12bx - 2[2ax - bx - 4ax - 2bx]$; $4ax - 12bx - 4ax + 2bx + 8ax + 4bx$; $8ax - 6bx$

page 37

Four times what number equals sixteen?

$4n = 16$

What number plus seven equals fifteen?

$n + 7 = 15$

A number divided by six minus four equals twelve.

$\frac{n}{6} - 4 = 12$

A number minus sixteen equals two.

$n - 16 = 2$

Three times what number plus seven equals thirteen?

$3n + 7 = 13$

A number divided in half plus fourteen equals twenty.

$\frac{n}{2} + 14 = 20$

page 38

Twice a number minus six equals the number plus seven

$2n - 6 = n + 7$

The product of five and a number equals one half the number plus eighteen.

$5n = \frac{n}{2} + 18$

Four-fifths of what number plus sixteen equals twenty-four.

$\frac{4}{5}n + 16 = 24$

A number plus fifteen is equal to twice the number minus eight.

$n + 15 = 2n - 8$

Two times the sum of a number and six equals eighteen.

$2(n + 6) = 18$

Four times a number minus one half the number equals twenty one.

$4n - \frac{n}{2} = 21$

0-88012-487-3

page 39

Eighteen minus the product of four and a number equals ten.

$18 - 4n = 10$

Twenty-six is equal to a number divided by five plus seven.

$26 = \frac{n}{5} + 7$

Three times a number plus six times that same number equals twenty-four.

$3n + 6n = 24$

Four times the sum of a number plus six equals thirty.

$4(n+6) = 30$

A number minus four and one-third equals eight.

$n - 4\frac{1}{3} = 8$

Seven times a number divided by three minus six equals three times the number.

$\frac{7n}{3} - 6 = 3n$

page 40

Check 6 + n = 8 for

n = 6
$6+n=8$
$6+(6)=8$
$12 \neq 8$

(n = 2)
$6+n=8$
$6+(2)=8$
$8=8$

Check n + 5 = 14 for:

n = 8
$n+5=14$
$(8)+5=14$
$13 \neq 14$

(n = 9)
$n+5=14$
$(9)+5=14$
$14=14$

Check n 8 = 2 for:

n = 12
$n-8=2$
$12-8=2$
$4 \neq 2$

(n = 10)
$n-8=2$
$10-8=2$
$2=2$

page 41

Check 3n + 5n 16 for

n 3
$3n+5n=16$
$3(3)+5(3)=16$
$9+15=16$
$24 \neq 16$

(n = 2)
$3n+5n=16$
$3(2)+5(2)=16$
$6+10=16$
$16=16$

Check 5n + n = 18 for

n = 2
$5n+n=18$
$5(2)+2=18$
$10+2=18$
$12 \neq 18$

(n = 3)
$5n+n=18$
$5(3)+3=18$
$15+3=18$
$18=18$

Check 3n + 7n = 30 for

(n = 3)
$3n+7n=30$
$3(3)+7(3)=30$
$9+21=30$
$30=30$

n = 10
$3n+7n=30$
$3(10)+7(10)=30$
$30+70=30$
$100 \neq 30$

page 42

+	7	8	1	0	3
2	16	18	4	2	8
6	20	22	8	6	12
5	19	21	7	5	11
9	23	25	11	9	15
4	18	20	6	4	10

page 43

Check $3n + \frac{n}{4} = 26$ for:

(n 8)
$3n+\frac{n}{4}=26$
$3(8)+\frac{(8)}{4}=26$
$24+2=26$
$26=26$

n = 12
$3n+\frac{n}{4}=26$
$3(12)+\frac{(12)}{4}=26$
$36+3=26$
$39 \neq 26$

Check $\frac{n}{2} + 4 = 8$ for

(n = 8)
$\frac{n}{2}+4=8$
$\frac{(8)}{2}+4=8$
$4+4=8$
$8=8$

n = 10
$\frac{n}{2}+4=8$
$\frac{(10)}{2}+4=8$
$5+4=8$
$9 \neq 8$

Check 3(n + 6) = 30 for:

(n = 4)
$3(n+6)=30$
$3(4+6)=30$
$3(10)=30$
$30=30$

n = 5
$3(n+6)=30$
$3(5+6)=30$
$3(11)=30$
$33 \neq 30$

Check 2(8 n) = 4 for:

n = 5
$2(8-n)=4$
$2(8-5)=4$
$2(3)=4$
$6 \neq 4$

(n = 6)
$2(8-n)=4$
$2(8-6)=4$
$2(2)=4$
$4=4$

page 44

3	2			4	4
6		6	7		8
	1	2		1	
8	6		2	6	

page 45

$1.5\ell + n = 2.5\ell$
$(-1.5\ell) \quad (-1.5\ell)$
$n = 1.0\ell$

$n = 3\text{ lb.} + 2\text{ lb.}$
$n = 5\text{ lb.}$

$5'2'' + n = 5'4''$
$(-5'2'') \quad (-5'2'')$
$n = 2''$

page 46

n 3 7
$n=7+3$
$n=10$

n 2 9
$n=9+2$
$n=11$

n 15 6
$n=6+15$
$n=21$

10 n 5
$10+5=n$
$15=n$

10 n 8
$10+8=n$
$18=n$

n 3 18
$n=18+3$
$n=21$

n 6 12
$n=12+6$
$n=18$

a 15 0
$a=0+15$
$a=15$

b 9 3
$b=3+9$
$b=12$

page 47

n 5 12
$n=12+5$
$n=17$

a 13 = 7
$a=7+13$
$a=20$

n 20 = 5
$n=5+20$
$n=25$

n 40 = 10
$n=10+40$
$n=50$

b 2 17
$b=17+2$
$b=19$

20 = n 16
$20+16=n$
$36=n$

18 = a 4
$18+4=a$
$22=a$

b 12 = 12
$b=12+12$
$b=24$

n 15 = 13
$n=13+15$
$n=28$

page 48

+	8	4	0	6	2
7	59	31	3	45	17
3	27	15	3	21	9
9	75	39	3	57	21
5	43	23	3	33	13
1	11	7	3	9	5

page 49

n + 7 11
$n=11-7$
$n=4$

n + 3 = 12
$n=12-3$
$n=9$

n + 10 22
$n=22-10$
$n=12$

n + 7 = 8
$n=8-7$
$n=1$

n + 15 20
$n=20-15$
$n=5$

n + 2 = 7
$n=7-2$
$n=5$

n + 5 5
$n=5-5$
$n=0$

n + 1 = 5
$n=5-1$
$n=4$

n + 12 = 15
$n=15-12$
$n=3$

page 50

n + 6 17
$n=17-6$
$n=11$

n + 5 46
$n=46-5$
$n=41$

n + 13 15
$n=15-13$
$n=2$

27 n + 8
$27-8=n$
$19=n$

14 a + 6
$14-6=a$
$8=a$

b + 4 18
$b=18-4$
$b=14$

n + 11 25
$n=25-11$
$n=14$

a + 7 35
$a=35-7$
$a=28$

n + 24 30
$n=30-24$
$n=6$

Solutions

0-88012-487-3

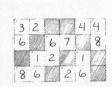

Solutions

page 51

$4n = \$4.88$
$n = \$1.22$

3 friends
\$3.66 total
n per share
$3n = \$3.66$
$n = \$1.22$ per share

n friends
\$5.95 total
\$1.19 per share
$n \times \$1.19 = \$5.95$
$n = 5$ friends

n friends
\$3.28 total
\$1.64 per share
$n \times \$1.64 = \$3.28$
$n = 2$ friends

n friends
\$7.26 total
\$1.21 per share
$n \times \$1.21 = \$7.26$
$n = 6$ friends

8 friends
\$9.68 total
n per share
$8n = \$9.68$
$n = \$1.21$ per share

7 friends
n total
\$1.51 per share
$n = 7 \times \$1.51$
$n = \$10.57$ total

page 52

$10n = 80$, $n = \frac{80}{10}$, $n = 8$

$4b = 84$, $b = \frac{84}{4}$, $b = 21$

$6a = 42$, $a = \frac{42}{6}$, $a = 7$

$8n = 40$, $n = \frac{40}{8}$, $n = 5$

$9b = 54$, $b = \frac{54}{9}$, $b = 6$

$15n = 45$, $n = \frac{45}{15}$, $n = 3$

$14a = 28$, $a = \frac{28}{14}$, $a = 2$

$5n = 15$, $n = \frac{15}{3}$, $n = 5$

$6n = 24$, $n = \frac{24}{6}$, $n = 4$

page 53

$\frac{n}{5} = 2$, $n = (5) \times 2$, $n = 10$

$\frac{n}{8} = 4$, $n = (8) \times 4$, $n = 32$

$\frac{n}{10} = 4$, $n = (10) \times 4$, $n = 40$

$\frac{a}{6} = 8$, $a = (6) \times 8$, $a = 48$

$\frac{n}{3} = 12$, $n = (3) \times 12$, $n = 36$

$\frac{b}{5} = 9$, $b = (5) \times 9$, $b = 45$

$\frac{b}{6} = 8$, $b = (6) \times 8$, $b = 48$

$\frac{n}{4} = 2$, $n = (4) \times 2$, $n = 8$

$\frac{c}{10} = 20$, $c = (10) \times 20$, $c = 200$

page 54

page 55

$\frac{n}{3} = 5$, $n = (3) \times 5$, $n = 15$

$\frac{n}{5} = 6$, $n = (5) \times 6$, $n = 30$

$\frac{n}{7} = 7$, $n = (7) \times 7$, $n = 49$

$\frac{n}{9} = 10$, $n = (9) \times 10$, $n = 90$

$\frac{n}{12} = 5$, $n = (12) \times 5$, $n = 60$

$\frac{n}{4} = 7$, $n = (4) \times 7$, $n = 28$

$\frac{n}{8} = 2$, $n = (8) \times 2$, $n = 16$

$\frac{n}{3} = 4$, $n = (3) \times 4$, $n = 12$

$\frac{n}{5} = 25$, $n = (5) \times 25$, $n = 125$

page 56

$3a = 12$, $a = \frac{12}{(3)}$, $a = 4$

$\frac{n}{6} = 3$, $n = (6) \times 3$, $n = 18$

$n - 5 = 8$, $n = (5) + 8$, $n = 13$

$n + 3 = 10$, $n = 10 - (3)$, $n = 7$

$\frac{b}{4} = 5$, $b = (4) \times 5$, $b = 20$

$4y = 24$, $y = \frac{24}{(4)}$, $y = 6$

$5n = 30$, $n = \frac{30}{(5)}$, $n = 6$

$b + 12 = 15$, $b = 15 - (12)$, $b = 3$

$n - 8 = 2$, $n = (8) + 2$, $n = 10$

$\frac{c}{5} = 9$, $c = (5) \times 9$, $c = 45$

page 57

$n = 1.4m - 1.2m$
$n = .2m$

$n = 4pr. + 2pr.$
$n = 6$ pairs

$n = 3.5m + .5m$
$n = 4m$

page 58

$n + 4 = 5$, $n = 5 - (4)$, $n = 1$

$9a = 81$, $a = \frac{81}{(9)}$, $a = 9$

$\frac{b}{8} = 9$, $b = (8) \times 9$, $b = 72$

$n - 7 = 16$, $n = (7) + 16$, $n = 23$

$a - 8 = 10$, $a = (8) + 10$, $a = 18$

$\frac{c}{8} = 3$, $c = (8) \times 3$, $c = 24$

$7c = 56$, $c = \frac{56}{(7)}$, $c = 8$

$n + 5 = 52$, $n = 52 - (5)$, $n = 47$

$b - 12 = 4$, $b = (12) + 4$, $b = 16$

$12n = 72$, $n = \frac{72}{(12)}$, $n = 6$

page 59

$n - 6 = 12$, $n = (6) + 12$, $n = 18$

$a + 2 = 30$, $a = 30 - (2)$, $a = 28$

$10a = 70$, $a = \frac{70}{(10)}$, $a = 7$

$\frac{b}{10} = 12$, $b = (10) \times 12$, $b = 120$

$\frac{n}{3} = 9$, $n = (3) \times 9$, $n = 27$

$n - 7 = 4$, $n = (7) + 4$, $n = 11$

$b + 30 = 40$, $b = 40 - (30)$, $b = 10$

$6n = 48$, $n = \frac{48}{(6)}$, $n = 8$

$4n = 44$, $n = \frac{44}{(4)}$, $n = 11$

$\frac{n}{15} = 2$, $n = (15) \times 2$, $n = 30$

page 60

$n = 12 \times \$2.00$
$n = \$24.00$

4 baskets
\$2.00 per basket
n profit
$n = 4 \times \$2.00$
$n = \$8.00$ profit

n baskets
\$1.00 per basket
\$15.00 profit
$\$1.00 \times n = \$15.00$
$n = 15$ baskets

n baskets
\$3.00 per basket
\$27.00 profit
$n \times \$3.00 = \$27.00$
$n = 9$ baskets

6 baskets
n per basket
\$18.00 profit
$6n = \$18.00$
$n = \$3.00$ per basket

7 baskets
\$2.00 per basket
n profit
$n = 7 \times \$2.00$
$n = \$14.00$ profit

4 baskets
n per basket
\$8.00 profit
$4n = \$8.00$
$n = \$2.00$ per basket

page 61

$6n = 20$, $n = \frac{20}{(6)}$, $n = 3\frac{1}{3}$

$a + 12 = 52$, $a = 52 - (12)$, $a = 40$

$n - 5 = 22$, $n = (5) + 22$, $n = 27$

$\frac{b}{5} = 13$, $b = (5) \times 13$, $b = 65$

$\frac{n}{2} = 23$, $n = (2) \times 23$, $n = 46$

$3a = 16$, $a = \frac{16}{(3)}$, $a = 5\frac{1}{3}$

$b + 11 = 25$, $b = 25 - (11)$, $b = 14$

$a + 5 = 9$, $a = 9 - (5)$, $a = 4$

$7y = 63$, $y = \frac{63}{(7)}$, $y = 9$

$c - 9 = 5$, $c = (9) + 5$, $c = 14$

page 62

$5a - 4 = 11$
$5a = 11 + (4)$
$5a = 15$
$a = \frac{15}{(5)}$
$a = 3$

$6b - 8 = 16$
$6b = 16 + (8)$
$6b = 24$
$b = \frac{24}{(6)}$
$b = 4$

$3n + 4 = 22$
$3n = 22 - (4)$
$3n = 18$
$n = \frac{18}{(3)}$
$n = 6$

$7y + 6 = 41$
$7y = 41 - (6)$
$7y = 35$
$y = \frac{35}{(7)}$
$y = 5$

page 63

$\frac{a}{3}+10=13$
$\frac{a}{3}=13-(10)$
$\frac{a}{3}=3$
$a=(3)\times 3$
$a=9$

$\frac{n}{5}+4=6$
$\frac{n}{5}=6-(4)$
$\frac{n}{5}=2$
$n=(5)\times 2$
$n=10$

$\frac{b}{2}-1=3$
$\frac{b}{2}=3+(1)$
$\frac{b}{2}=4$
$b=(2)\times 4$
$b=8$

$\frac{n}{4}-3=2$
$\frac{n}{4}=2+(3)$
$\frac{n}{4}=5$
$n=(4)\times 5$
$n=20$

page 64

5

Tally

X = 4	||
X = 5	||||
X = 6	|||
X = 7	|

page 65

$6n+8=32$
$6n=32-(8)$
$6n=24$
$n=\frac{24}{(6)}$
$n=4$

$12+\frac{n}{3}=17$
$\frac{n}{3}=17-(12)$
$\frac{n}{3}=5$
$n=(3)\times 5$
$n=15$

$\frac{a}{3}+10=11$
$\frac{a}{3}=11-(10)$
$\frac{a}{3}=1$
$a=(3)\times 1$
$a=3$

$9a-18=9$
$9a=(18)+9$
$9a=27$
$a=\frac{27}{(9)}$
$a=3$

$4+5a=19$
$5a=19-(4)$
$5a=15$
$a=\frac{15}{(5)}$
$a=3$

$\frac{b}{4}-3=3$
$\frac{b}{4}=(3)+3$
$\frac{b}{4}=6$
$b=(4)\times 6$
$b=24$

page 66

$6a+5=7$
$6a=7-(5)$
$6a=2$
$a=\frac{2}{(6)}$
$a=\frac{1}{3}$

$\frac{n}{4}+3\frac{1}{4}=7$
$\frac{n}{4}=7-(3\frac{1}{4})$
$\frac{n}{4}=3\frac{3}{4}$
$n=(4)\times 3\frac{3}{4}$
$n=15$

$\frac{n}{9}+6=6\frac{1}{3}$
$\frac{n}{9}=6\frac{1}{3}-(6)$
$\frac{n}{9}=\frac{1}{3}$
$n=(9)\times\frac{1}{3}$
$n=\frac{9}{3}=3$

$5a+12=14$
$5a=14-(12)$
$5a=2$
$a=\frac{2}{(5)}$
$a=\frac{2}{5}$

$4b-25=15$
$4b=(25)+15$
$4b=40$
$b=\frac{40}{4}$
$b=10$

$\frac{a}{4}-2\frac{1}{2}=4$
$\frac{a}{4}=(2\frac{1}{2})+4$
$\frac{a}{4}=6\frac{1}{2}$
$a=(4)\times 6\frac{1}{2}$
$a=26$

page 67

9

Tally

X 6	||
X 7	|
X 8	|||
X 9	||||

page 68

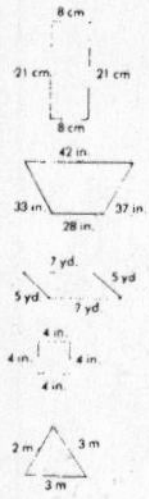

P = 21+8+21+8 = 58 cm or 2(8+21) = 58 cm

P = 33+42+37+28 = 140 in.

P = 5+7+5+7 = 24 yd or 2(5+7) = 24 yd.

P = 4+4+4+4 = 16 in. or 4 × 4 in. = 16 in.

P = 2+3+3 = 8 m

page 69

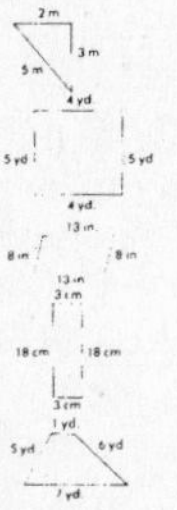

P = 5+2+3 = 10 m

P = 5+4+5+4 = 18 yd. or 2(5+4) = 18 yd.

P = 8+13+8+13 = 42 in. or 2(8+13) = 42 in.

P = 18+3+18+3 = 42 cm or 2(18+3) = 42 cm.

P = 5+1+6+7 = 19 yd.

page 70

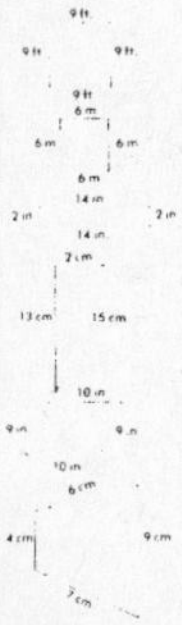

P = 9+9+9+9 = 36 ft or 4 × 9 ft = 36 ft

P = 6+6+6+6 = 24 m or 4 × 6 m = 24 m

P = 2+14+2+14 = 32 in. or 2(2+14) = 32 in.

P = 13+2+15 = 30 cm

P = 9+10+9+10 = 38 in. or 2(9+10) = 38 in.

P = 4+6+9+7 = 26 cm

page 71

1	1	5		1	4	4
0		0		1		0
0		1	0	2		0

page 72

d = 28 in.
$C=\frac{22}{7}\times\frac{28}{1}=88$
C = 88 in

d = 7 ft.
$C=\frac{22}{7}\times\frac{7}{1}=22$
C = 22 ft

r = 14 mm
d = 28 mm
$C=\frac{22}{7}\times\frac{28}{1}=88$
C = 88 mm

page 73

r = 21 in.
d = 42 in.
$C=\frac{22}{7}\times\frac{42}{1}=132$
C = 132 in.

r = 21 in.
d = 42 in.
3.14 × 42 = 628 + 1256
C = 131.88 in.

d = 35 cm
$C=\frac{22}{7}\times\frac{35}{1}=110$
C = 110 cm

d = 35 cm
3.14 × 35 = 1570 + 942
C = 109.90 cm

r = 3.5 ft.
d = 7 ft.
$C=\frac{22}{7}\times\frac{7}{1}=22$
C = 22 ft

r = 3.5 ft.
d = 7 ft.
3.14 × 7
C = 21.98 ft.

page 74

d = 14 in.
$C=\frac{22}{7}\times\frac{14}{1}=44$
C = 44 in.

d = 14 in.
3.14 × 14 = 1256 + 314
C = 43.96 in

r = 10.5 mm
d = 21 mm
$C=\frac{22}{7}\times\frac{21}{1}=66$
C = 66 mm

r = 10.5 mm
d = 21 mm
3.14 × 21 = 314 + 628
C = 65.94 mm

d = 10.5 ft.
$C=\frac{22}{7}\times\frac{21}{2}=33$
C = 33 ft

d = 10.5 ft.
3.14 × 10.5 = 1570 + 3140
C = 32.970 ft.

0-88012-487-3

Solutions

page 75

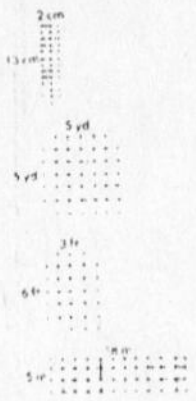

A = 13 cm × 2 cm
A = 26 sq cm

A = 5 yd × 5 yd
A = 25 sq yd

A = 3 ft × 6 ft
A = 18 sq ft.

A = 5 m × 18 m
A = 90 sq m

page 76

A = 14 yd × 3 yd
A = 42 sq yd

A = 2 m × 16 m
A = 32 sq m

A = 11 in × 11 in
A = 121 sq in.

A = 8 cm × 12 cm
A = 96 sq cm

page 77

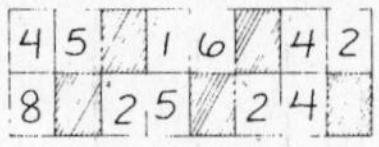

page 78

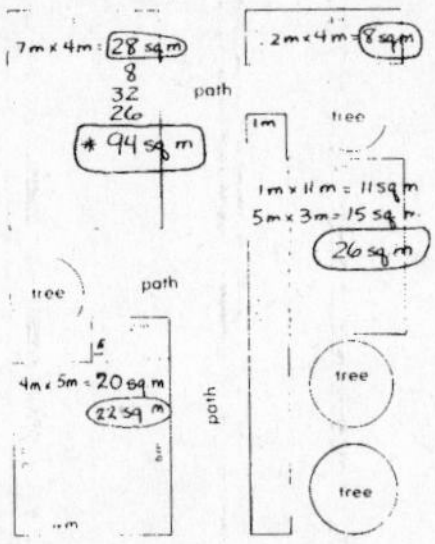

page 79

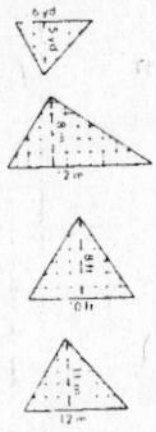

$A = \frac{1}{2}(6\text{ yd} \times 5\text{ yd})$
$A = \frac{1}{2}(30\text{ sq yd})$
A = 15 sq yd
$A = \frac{1}{2}(12\text{ m} \times 8\text{ m})$
$A = \frac{1}{2}(96\text{ sq m})$
A = 48 sq m

$A = \frac{1}{2}(10\text{ ft} \times 8\text{ ft})$
$A = \frac{1}{2}(80\text{ sq ft})$
A = 40 sq ft.

$A = \frac{1}{2}(12\text{ m} \times 11\text{ m})$
$A = \frac{1}{2}(132\text{ sq m})$
A = 66 sq m

page 80

$A = \frac{1}{2}(8\text{ cm} \times 2\text{ cm})$
$A = \frac{1}{2}(16\text{ sq cm})$
A = 8 sq cm
$A = \frac{1}{2}(7\text{ yd} \times 5\text{ yd})$
$A = \frac{1}{2}(35\text{ sq yd})$
$A = 17\frac{1}{2}$ sq yd
$A = \frac{1}{2}(9\text{ m} \times 7\text{ m})$
$A = \frac{1}{2}(63\text{ sq m})$
$A = 31\frac{1}{2}$ sq m

$A = \frac{1}{2}(11\text{ ft} \times 8\text{ ft})$
$A = \frac{1}{2}(88\text{ sq ft})$
A = 44 sq ft

page 81

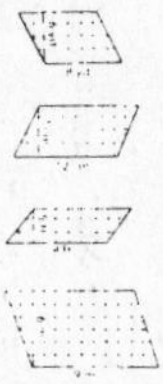

A = (8 yd × 6 yd)
A = 48 sq yd

A = (12 cm × 7 cm)
A = 84 sq cm

A = (8 ft × 5 ft)
A = 40 sq ft

A = (6 m × 9 m)
A = 54 sq m

page 82

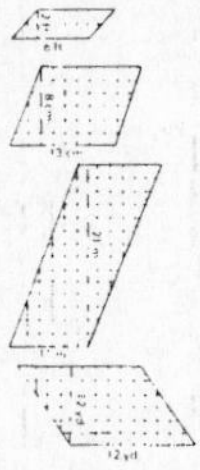

A = (6 ft × 2 ft)
A = 12 sq ft
A = (13 cm × 8 cm)
A = 104 sq cm

A = (11 m × 21 m)
A = 231 sq m

A = (12 yd × 12 yd)
A = 144 sq yd

page 83

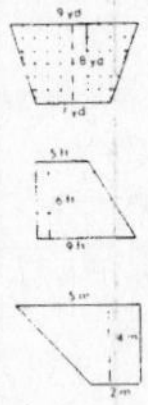

$A = \frac{9\text{ yd} + 7\text{ yd}}{2} \times \frac{8\text{ yd}}{1}$
A = 16 yd × 4 yd
A = 64 sq yd

$A = \frac{5\text{ ft} + 9\text{ ft}}{2} \times \frac{6\text{ ft}}{1}$
A = 14 ft × 3 ft
A = 42 sq ft.

$A = \frac{5\text{ m} + 2\text{ m}}{2} \times \frac{4\text{ m}}{1}$
A = 7 m × 2 m
A = 14 sq m

page 84

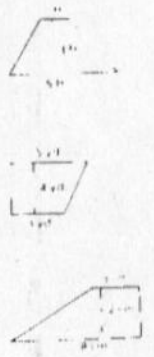

$A = \frac{1\text{ ft} + 5\text{ ft}}{2} \times \frac{3\text{ ft}}{1}$
$A = \frac{6\text{ ft}}{2} \times \frac{3\text{ ft}}{1}$
A = 3 ft × 3 ft
A = 9 sq ft.
$A = \frac{5\text{ yd} + 3\text{ yd}}{2} \times \frac{4\text{ yd}}{1}$
$A = \frac{8\text{ yd}}{2} \times \frac{4\text{ yd}}{1}$
A = 4 yd × 4 yd
A = 16 sq yd.
$A = \frac{3\text{ cm} + 8\text{ cm}}{2} \times \frac{2\text{ cm}}{1}$
A = 11 cm × 1 cm
A = 11 sq cm

page 85

$A = \frac{22}{7} \times \frac{7\text{ in}}{1} \times \frac{7\text{ in}}{1}$
A = 154 sq in.

$A = \frac{22}{7} \times \frac{21\text{ m}}{2} \times \frac{21\text{ m}}{2}$
$A = \frac{693}{2}$ sq m
$A = 346\frac{1}{2}$ sq m
$A = \frac{22}{7} \times \frac{3\text{ ft}}{1} \times \frac{3\text{ ft}}{1}$
$A = \frac{198}{7}$ sq ft
$A = 28\frac{2}{7}$ sq ft

page 86

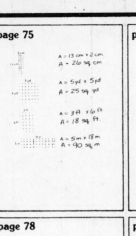

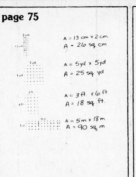

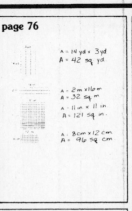

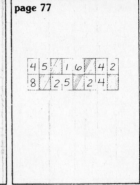

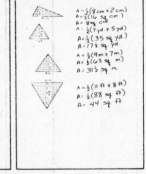

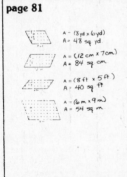

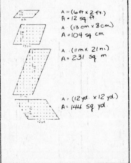

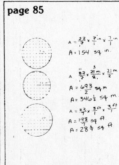

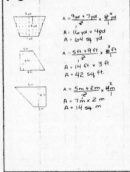

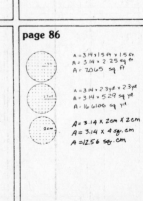

A = 3.14 × 1.5 ft × 1.5 ft
A = 3.14 × 2.25 sq ft
A = 7.065 sq ft

A = 3.14 × 2.3 yd × 2.3 yd
A = 3.14 × 5.29 sq yd
A = 16.6106 sq yd

A = 3.14 × 2 cm × 2 cm
A = 3.14 × 4 sq. cm
A = 12.56 sq. cm

0-88012-487-3

Equations

Check the Equations

Check $3n + \frac{n}{4} = 26$ for:

$n = 8$ $n = 12$

Check $\frac{n}{2} + 4 = 8$ for:

$n = 8$ $n = 10$

Check $3(n + 6) = 30$ for:

$n = 4$ $n = 5$

Check $2(8 - n) = 4$ for:

$n = 5$ $n = 6$

0-88012-487-3

Equation Crossword

Solve the equations using these values:

$a = 10; b = 2; c = 3$

Then write your answers in the cross number puzzle below.

across:

1. $3a + b =$
2. $4a + 2b =$
4. $6a + 2b + c =$
5. $a + b =$
7. $7a + 8b =$
8. $2a + 2c =$

down:

1. $3a + 3b =$
3. $4a + 4b =$
4. $6a + b =$
5. $8b =$
6. $a + 2c =$

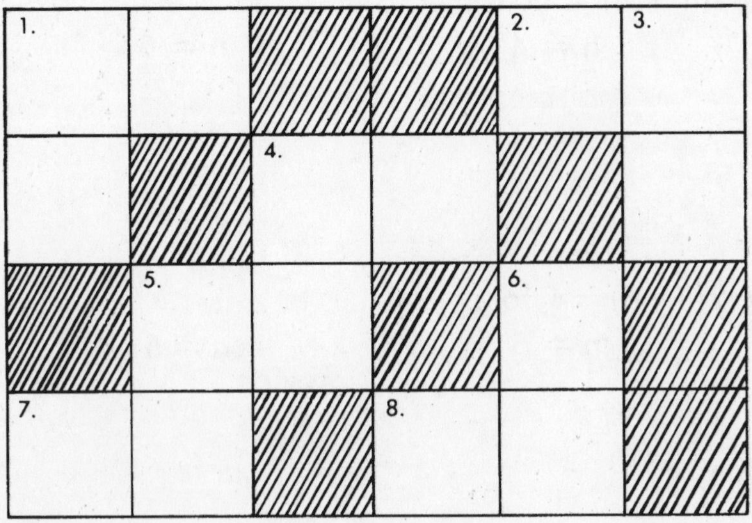

0-88012-487-3

Word Problems

Equation Solving

Write and solve algebraic equations for the following situations:

Mrs. Williams wants to fill a 2.5 liter jug with lemonade. She has made 1.5 liters. How much more must she make?

Mr. Franklin put three pounds of bacon in his shopping cart. Later, he went back for two more. How many pounds of bacon did he buy?

Aretha is 5′2″; her mother is 5′4″. How much must Aretha grow in order to be as tall as her mother?

0-88012-487-3

Equations

Solve the Equations

$n-8=4$
$n=4+8$
$n=12$

$n-3=7$

$n-2=9$

$n-15=6$

$10=n-5$

$10=n-8$

$n-3=18$

$n-6=12$

$a-15=0$

$b-9=3$

0-88012-487-3

Equations

Solve the Equations

$n - 3 = 16$
$n = 16 + 3$
$n = 19$

$n - 5 = 12$

$a - 13 = 7$

$n - 20 = 5$

$n - 40 = 10$

$b - 2 = 17$

$20 = n - 16$

$18 = a - 4$

$b - 12 = 12$

$n - 15 = 13$

0-88012-487-3

Number Table

Complete the table.

Using the values given for x, y or the solutions, find the missing numbers.

x (across the top) / y (down the side)

$x \cdot y + 3 =$	8			6	2
	59			45	17
3		15	3		
				57	
5	43			33	
1			3		5

0-88012-487-3

Equations

Solve the Equations

$n + 4 = 10$
$n = 10 - 4$
$n = 6$

an example

$n + 7 = 11$

$n + 3 = 12$

$n + 10 = 22$

$n + 7 = 8$

$n + 15 = 20$

$n + 2 = 7$

$n + 5 = 5$

$n + 1 = 5$

$n + 12 = 15$

0-88012-487-3

Equations

Solve the Equations

$n + 22 = 30$
$n = 30 - 22$
$n = 8$

$n + 6 = 17$

$n + 5 = 46$

$n + 13 = 15$

$27 = n + 8$

$14 = a + 6$

$b + 4 = 18$

$n + 11 = 25$

$a + 7 = 35$

$n + 24 = 30$

0-88012-487-3

Word Problems

Equation Solving

Four friends ate at the Hamburger Joint. Each person had two hamburgers, and they shared a large pitcher of H–J Cola and some French fries. The total bill was $4.88 including tax. Write and solve an equation that shows how much each person owes.

Write and solve equations for each of the following situations:

3 friends
$3.66 total
n per share

n friends
$5.95 total
$1.19 per share

n friends
$3.28 total
$1.64 per share

n friends
$7.26 total
$1.21 per share

8 friends
$9.68 total
n per share

7 friends
n total
$1.51 per share

 0-88012-487-3

Equations

Solve the Equations

$$7n = 63$$
$$n = \frac{63}{7}$$
$$n = 9$$

$10n = 80$

$4b = 84$

$6a = 42$

$8n = 40$

$9b = 54$

$15n = 45$

$14a = 28$

$5n = 15$

$6n = 24$

0-88012-487-3

Equations

Solve the Equations

$\frac{n}{6} = 3$
$n = (6) \times 3$
$n = 18$

$\frac{n}{5} = 2$

$\frac{n}{8} = 4$

$\frac{n}{10} = 4$

$\frac{a}{6} = 8$

$\frac{n}{3} = 12$

$\frac{b}{5} = 9$

$\frac{b}{6} = 8$

$\frac{n}{4} = 2$

$\frac{c}{10} = 20$

0-88012-487-3

Equation Crossword

Solve the equations using these values:

$a = 20;\ b = 4;\ c = 1$

Then write your answers in the cross number puzzle below.

across:

1. $a + b + c =$
3. $3a + 2b =$
5. $a + 2b + c =$
7. $2a + 2b =$
10. $a + 3c =$
12. $a - (b + c) =$

down:

2. $2a + 3b =$
4. $4a + b =$
6. $5a - 2b =$
8. $5a - 3b =$
9. $3a - 9c =$
11. $2a - 2c =$

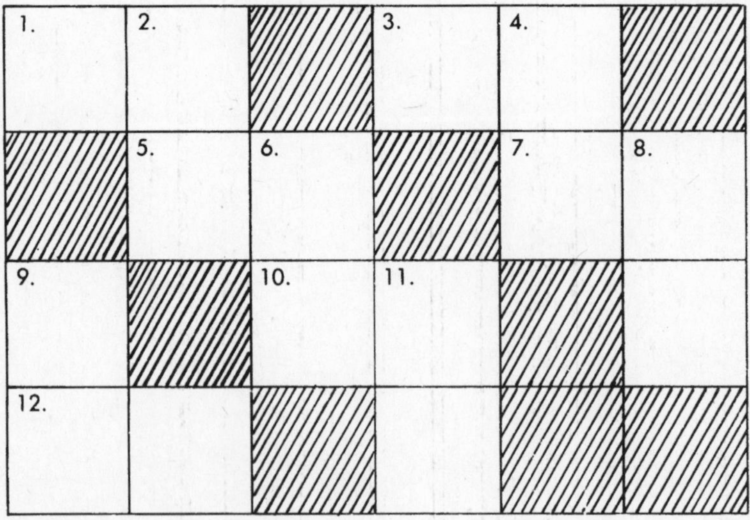

 0-88012-487-3

Equations

Solve the Equations

$\frac{n}{4} = 4$
$n = (4) \times 4$
$n = 16$

Your example

$\frac{n}{3} = 5$

$\frac{n}{5} = 6$

$\frac{n}{7} = 7$

$\frac{n}{9} = 10$

$\frac{n}{12} = 5$

$\frac{n}{4} = 7$

$\frac{n}{8} = 2$

$\frac{n}{3} = 4$

$\frac{n}{5} = 25$

0-88012-487-3

Equations

Solve the Equations

$3a = 12$

$\frac{n}{6} = 3$

$n - 5 = 8$

$n + 3 = 10$

$\frac{b}{4} = 5$

$4y = 24$

$5n = 30$

$b + 12 = 15$

$n - 8 = 2$

$\frac{c}{5} = 9$

0-88012-487-3

Word Problems

Equation Solving

Write and solve algebraic equations for the following situations.

Ralph has a board that is 1.4 m long. He needs a board that is 1.2 m long. How much should he cut off the board?

Jack had 4 pairs of jeans and bought two more pairs. How many pairs of jeans does Jack have?

A pattern calls for 3.5 meters of fabric. Janet wants to have .5 m extra to make a head scarf to match. How much fabric should she buy?

0-88012-487-3

Equations

Solve the Equations

$n + 4 = 5$

$9a = 81$

$\frac{b}{8} = 9$

$n - 7 = 16$

$a - 8 = 10$

$\frac{c}{8} = 3$

$7c = 56$

$n + 5 = 52$

$b - 12 = 4$

$12n = 72$

0-88012-487-3

Equations

Solve the Equations

$n-6=12$

$a+2=30$

$10a=70$

$\frac{b}{10}=12$

$\frac{n}{3}=9$

$n-7=4$

$b+30=40$

$6n=48$

$4n=44$

$\frac{n}{15}=2$

0-88012-487-3

Word Problems

Equation Solving

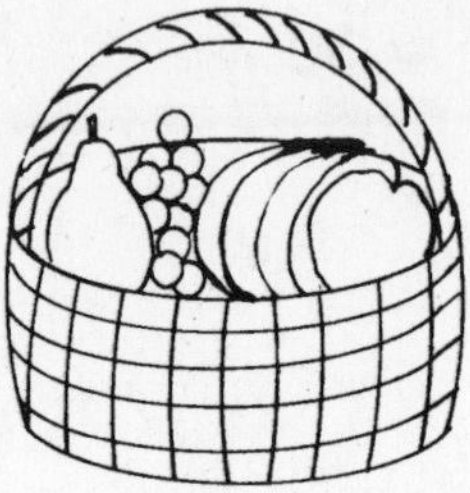

A club makes $2.00 profit on each fruit basket it sells. Write and solve an equation that shows how much Janet made for her club by selling 12 fruit baskets.

Write and solve equations for each of the following situations.

4 baskets
$2.00 per basket
n profit

n baskets
$1.00 per basket
$15.00 profit

n baskets
$3.00 per basket
$27.00 profit

6 baskets
n per basket
$18.00 profit

7 baskets
$2.00 per basket
n profit

4 baskets
n per basket
$8.00 profit

 0-88012-487-3

Equations

Solve the Equations

$6n = 20$

$a + 12 = 52$

$n - 5 = 22$

$\frac{b}{5} = 13$

$\frac{n}{2} = 23$

$3a = 16$

$b + 11 = 25$

$a + 5 = 9$

$7y = 63$

$c - 9 = 5$

0-88012-487-3

Equations

Solve the Equations

Solve the equations using two operations.

Study this first

$$3a - 2 = 13$$

$$3a + (2) - 2 = 13 + (2) \leftarrow \text{Operation \#1}$$

$$3a = 15$$

$$\frac{3a}{3} = \frac{15}{3} \leftarrow \text{Operation \#2}$$

$$a = 5$$

$5a - 4 = 11$

$6b - 8 = 16$

$3n + 4 = 22$

$7y + 6 = 41$

0-88012-487-3

Equations

Solve the Equations

Solve the equations using two operations.

$$\frac{b}{3} + 15 = 17$$

$$\frac{b}{3} + 15 - (15) = 17 - (15) \leftarrow \text{Operation\#1}$$

$$\frac{b}{3} = 2$$

$$(\cancel{3}) \times \frac{b}{\cancel{3}} = (3) \times 2 \leftarrow \text{Operation \#2}$$

$$b = 6$$

$\frac{a}{3} + 10 = 13$

$\frac{n}{5} + 4 = 6$

$\frac{b}{2} - 1 = 3$

$\frac{n}{4} - 3 = 2$

0-88012-487-3

Equations

What solution is named most often? ________

$2X + 1 = 9$

$3X + 2 = 2X + 7$

$\frac{2x}{3} = 4$

$2X - 3 = X + 2$

$13 - X = X - 1$

$29 - 3X = 11$

$16 - 2X = 2X$

$3 + X = 8$

$\frac{x}{2} = X - 3$

$5X = 25$

Tally

$X = 4$ ______

$X = 5$ ______

$X = 6$ ______

$X = 7$ ______

0-88012-487-3

Equations

Solve the Equations

Solve the equations using two operations.

$6n + 8 = 32$

$12 + \frac{n}{3} = 17$

$\frac{a}{3} + 10 = 11$

$9a - 18 = 9$

$4 + 5a = 19$

$\frac{b}{4} - 3 = 3$

0-88012-487-3

Equations

Solve the Equations

Solve the equations using two operations.

$6a + 5 = 7$

$\frac{n}{4} + 3\frac{1}{4} = 7$

$\frac{n}{9} + 6 = 6\frac{1}{3}$

$5a + 12 = 14$

$4b - 25 = 15$

$\frac{a}{4} - 2\frac{1}{2} = 4$

0-88012-487-3

Equations

What solution is named most often? ________

$\frac{x}{2} + 1 = 5$

$X - 3 = 6$

$X + 4 = 2X - 4$

$3X + 1 = 4 \times 7$

$\frac{x}{3} + 1 = 4$

$3X + 2 = 20$

$\frac{x}{4} + 2 = 4$

$3X + 5 = 26$

$2X = X + 6$

$2X + 1 = 19$

Tally

$X = 6$ ______

$X = 7$ ______

$X = 8$ ______

$X = 9$ ______

You have finished
Step 3

 0-88012-487-3

Perimeters

perimeter: distance around a plane figure.

P = sum of the sides

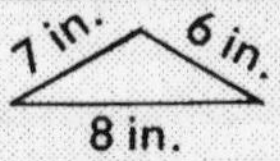

P = 7 in. + 6 in. +8 in. = 21 in.

Find the perimeter of each figure.

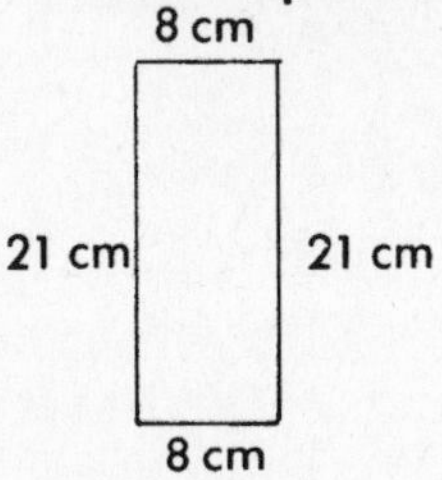

P =

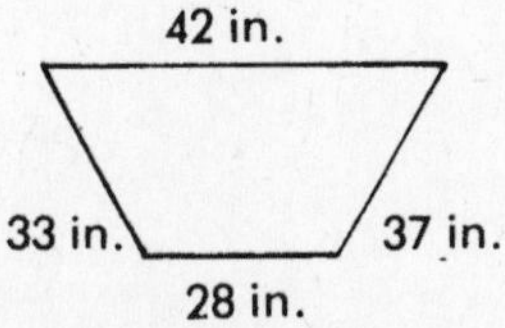

P =

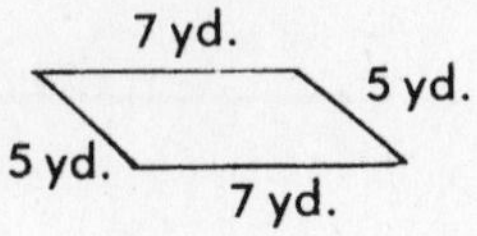

P =

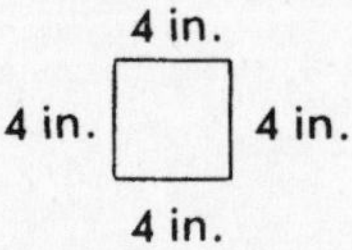

P =

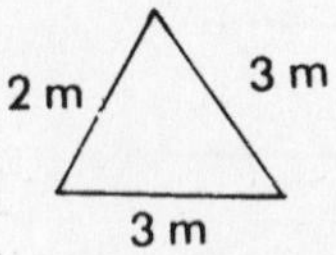

P =

 0-88012-487-3

Perimeters

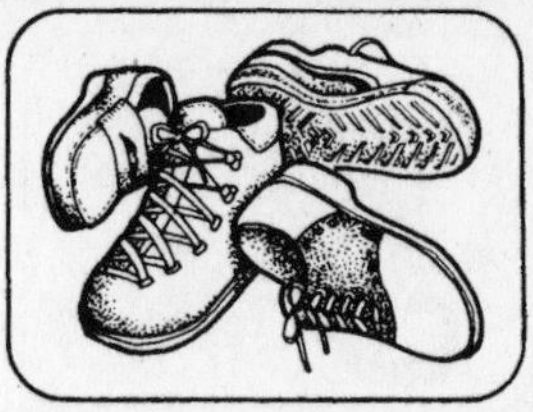

perimeter: distance around a plane figure.

P = sum of the sides.

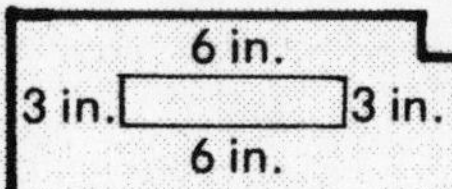

P = 3 in. + 6 in. +3 in. + 6 in. = 18 in.

Find the perimeter of each figure.

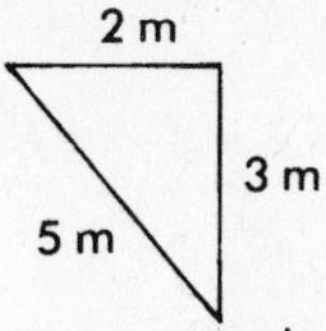

P =

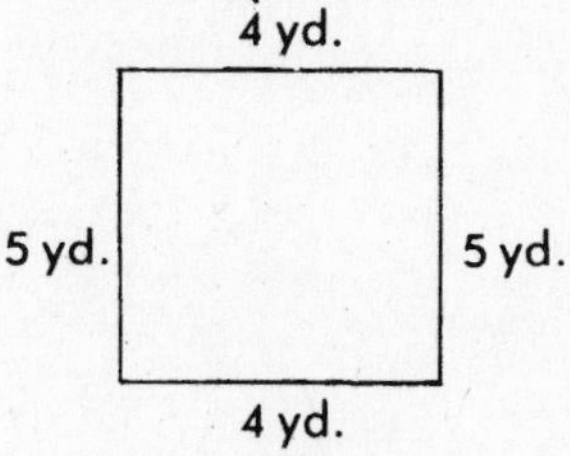

P =

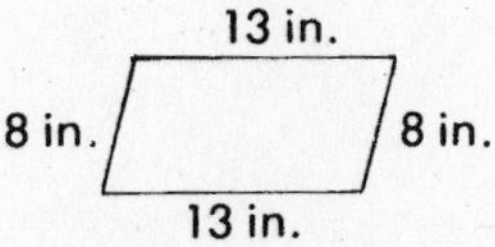

P =

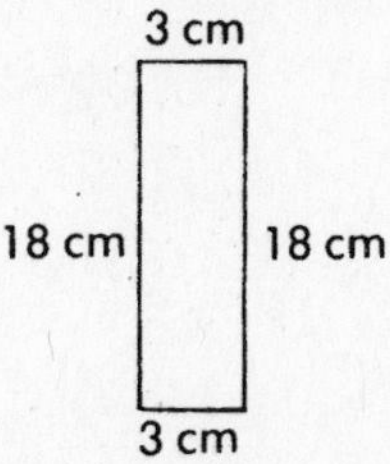

P =

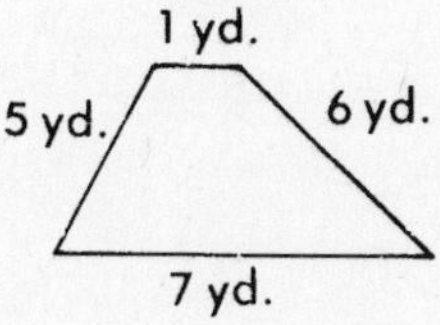

P =

0-88012-487-3

Perimeters

Find the perimeter of each figure.

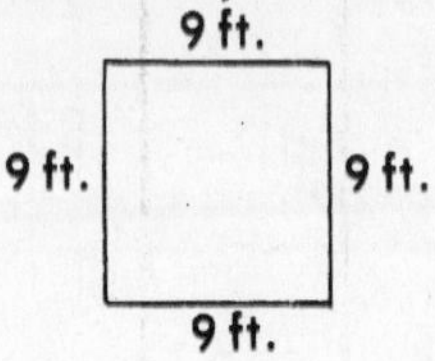

P =

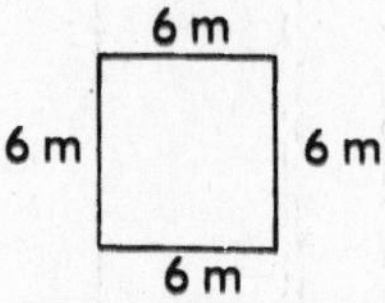

P =

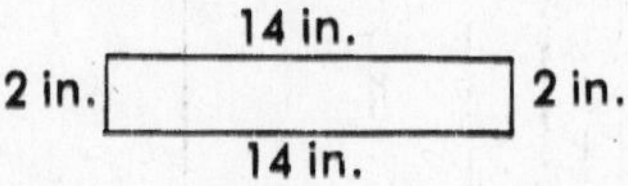

P =

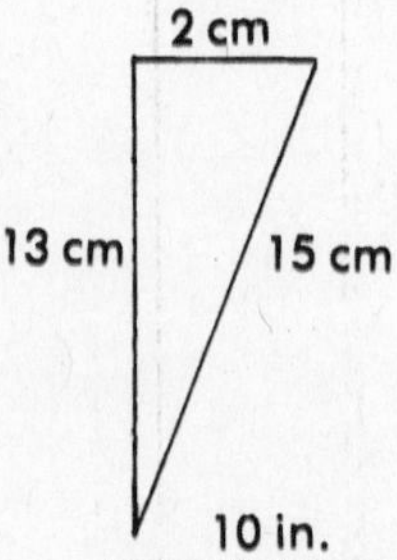

P =

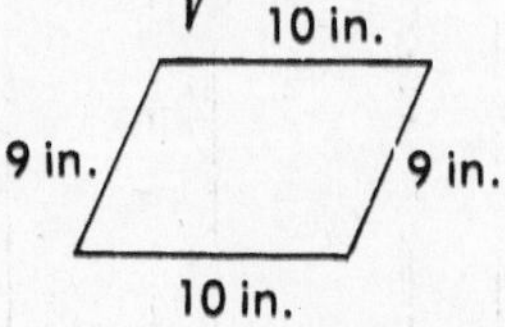

P =

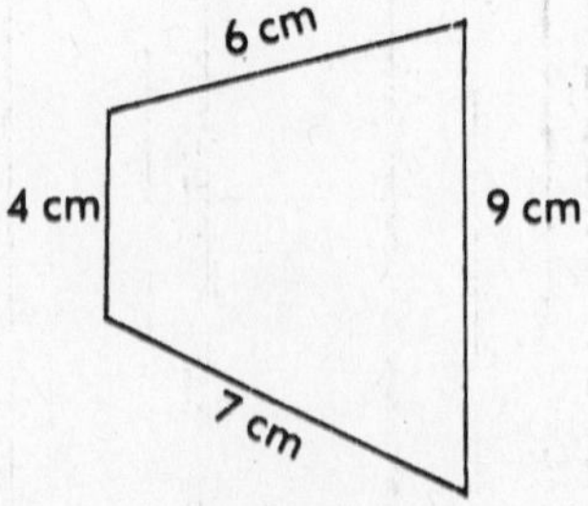

P =

 0-88012-487-3

Perimeter Crossword

Figure the perimeter of each figure. Then write your answers in the cross number puzzle below.

across:

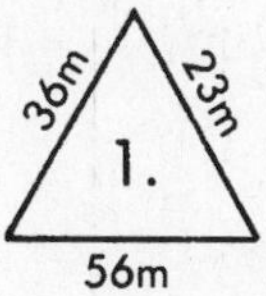

36m
23
+56
______
m

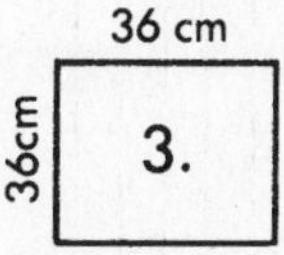

36cm
X 4
______
cm

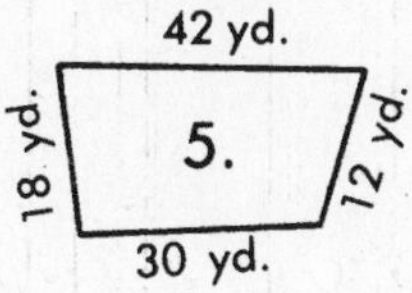

42 yd.
12
30
+18
______
yd.

down:

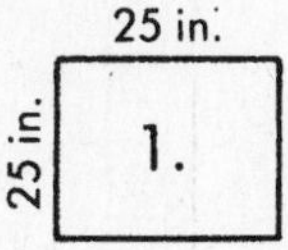

in.
______
in.

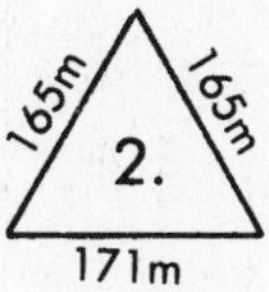

m
______
m

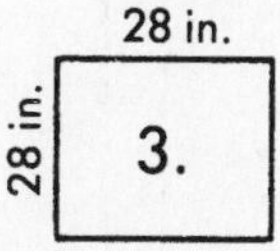

in.
______
in.

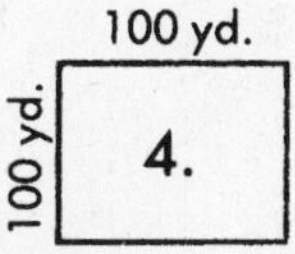

yd.
______
yd.

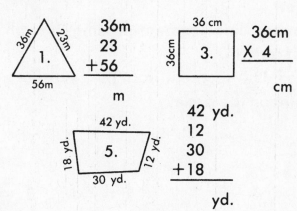

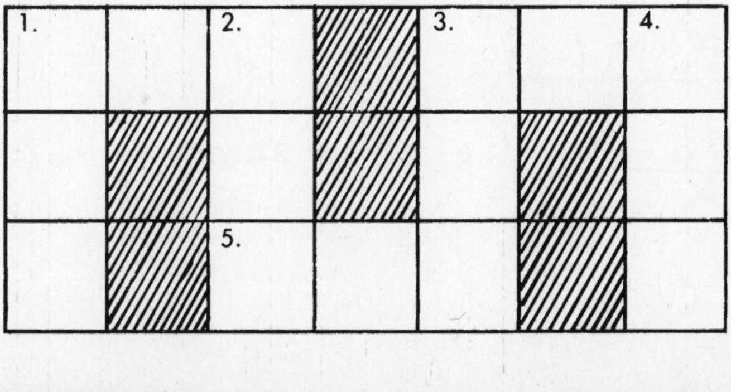

0-88012-487-3

Circumference

Perimeters

circumference: perimeter of, or distance around a circle.

diameter: line segment passing through the center of a circle.

radius: line segment from the center of a circle to a point on the circle.

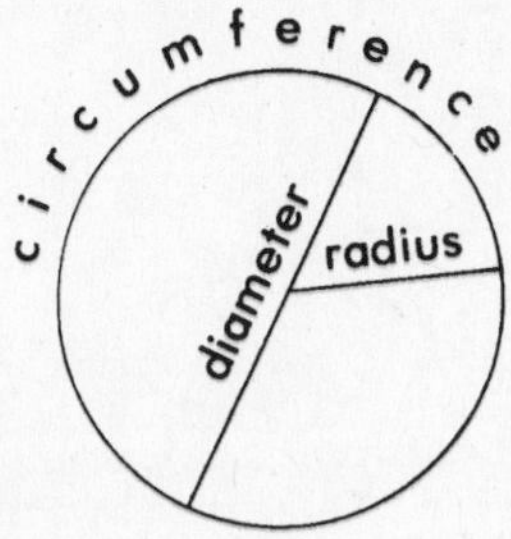

$c = \pi d$ $2r = d$

Find the circumference of each of these circles. Let $\pi = 22/7$

Here's an example

$r = 7$ mm
$d = 14$ mm
$c = \frac{22}{7} \times \frac{14}{1}$ mm (14 and 7 cancelled: 2)
$c = 44$ mm

$d = 28$ in.

$d = 7$ ft.

$r = 14$ mm

0-88012-487-3

Circumference

Perimeters

circumference: perimeter of, or distance around a circle.

$c = \pi d$ $d = 2r$

Find the circumference of each of these circles.

Let $\pi = 22/7$	Let $\pi = 3.14$
$r = 21$ in.	$r = 21$ in.
$d = 35$ cm	$d = 35$ cm
$r = 3\frac{1}{2}$ ft.	$r = 3.5$ ft.

0-88012-487-3

Circumference

Perimeters

circumference: perimeter of, or distance around a circle.

$c = \pi d$ $d = 2r$

Find the circumference of each of these circles.

Let $\pi = 22/7$	Let $\pi = 3.14$
$d = 14$ in.	$d = 14$ in.
$r = 10\frac{1}{2}$ mm	$r = 10.5$ mm
$d = 10\frac{1}{2}$ ft.	$d = 10.5$ ft.

 0-88012-487-3

Area

area: number of square units in a figure.

Area (of a rectangle) = length × width.

A = l × w

A = 5 ft. × 3 ft.

A = 15 sq. ft.

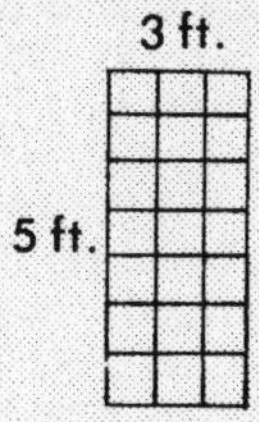

We did this one for you

Find the area of each rectangle.

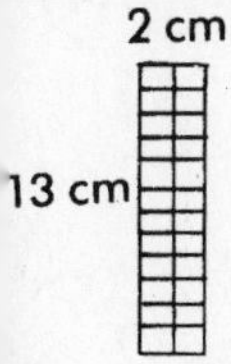

A =

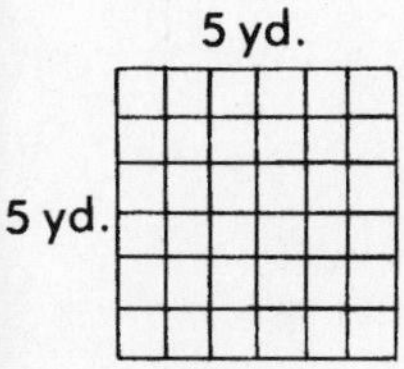

A =

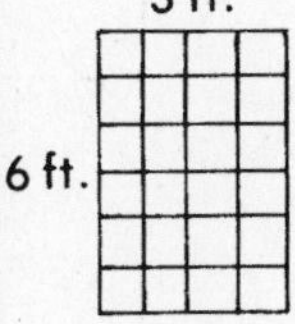

A =

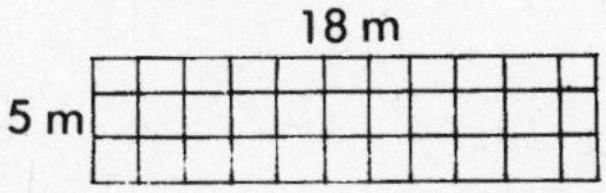

A =

 0-88012-487-3

Area

<u>area</u>: number of square units in a figure.
Area (of a rectangle) = length × width.

A = l × w

A = 3 m × 2 m

A = 6 sq. m

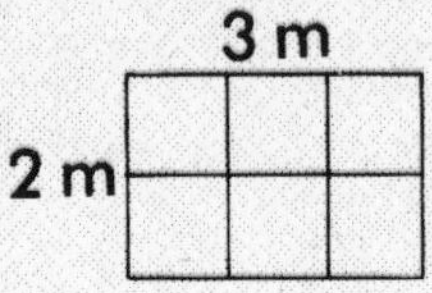

Find the area of each rectangle.

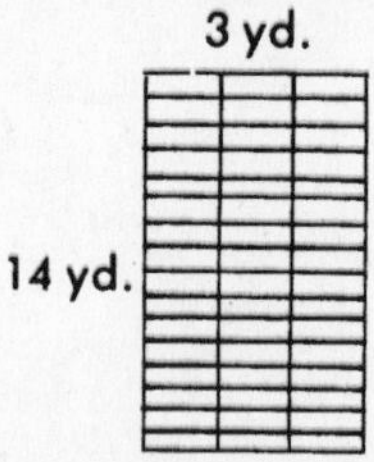

A =

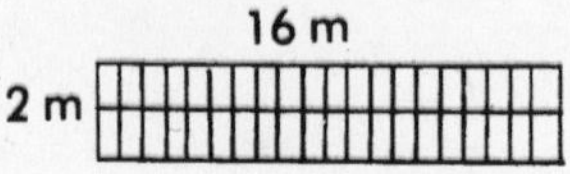

A =

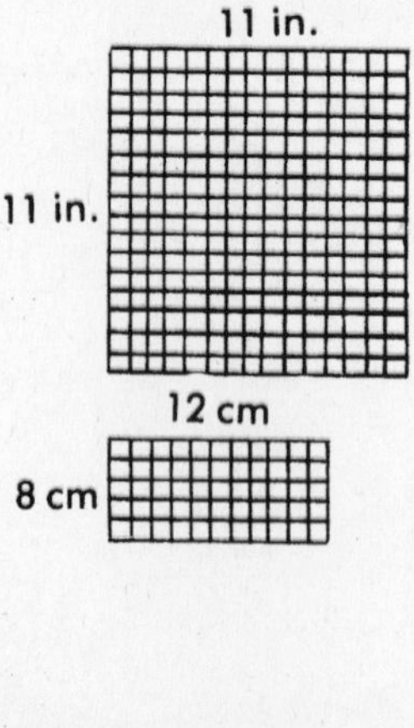

A =

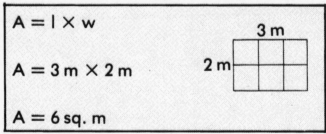

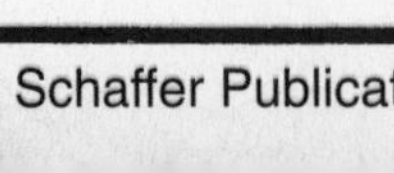

A =

0-88012-487-3

Area Crossword

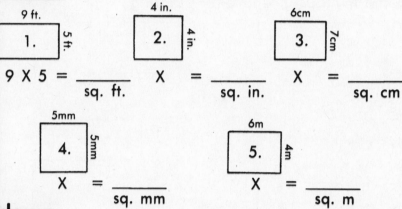

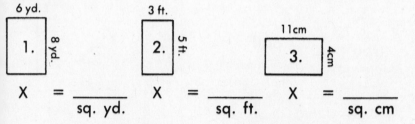

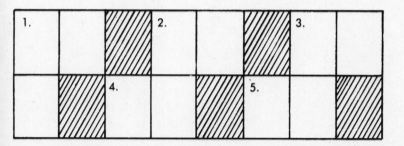

Figure the area of each rectangle. Then write your answers in the cross number puzzle below.

across:

1. 9 ft. × 5 ft.
$9 \times 5 =$ ______ sq. ft.

2. 4 in. × 4 in.
X = ______ sq. in.

3. 6cm × 7cm
X = ______ sq. cm

4. 5mm × 5mm
X = ______ sq. mm

5. 6m × 4m
X = ______ sq. m

down:

1. 6 yd. × 8 yd.
X = ______ sq. yd.

2. 3 ft. × 5 ft.
X = ______ sq. ft.

3. 11cm × 4cm
X = ______ sq. cm

1.		▨	2.		▨	3.	
	▨	4.		▨	5.		▨

0-88012-487-3

Flower Beds

The biggest job that Toni's Flower Bed business had was for a small park. The trees were already planted. Figure how many square meters Toni's company must prepare for planting.

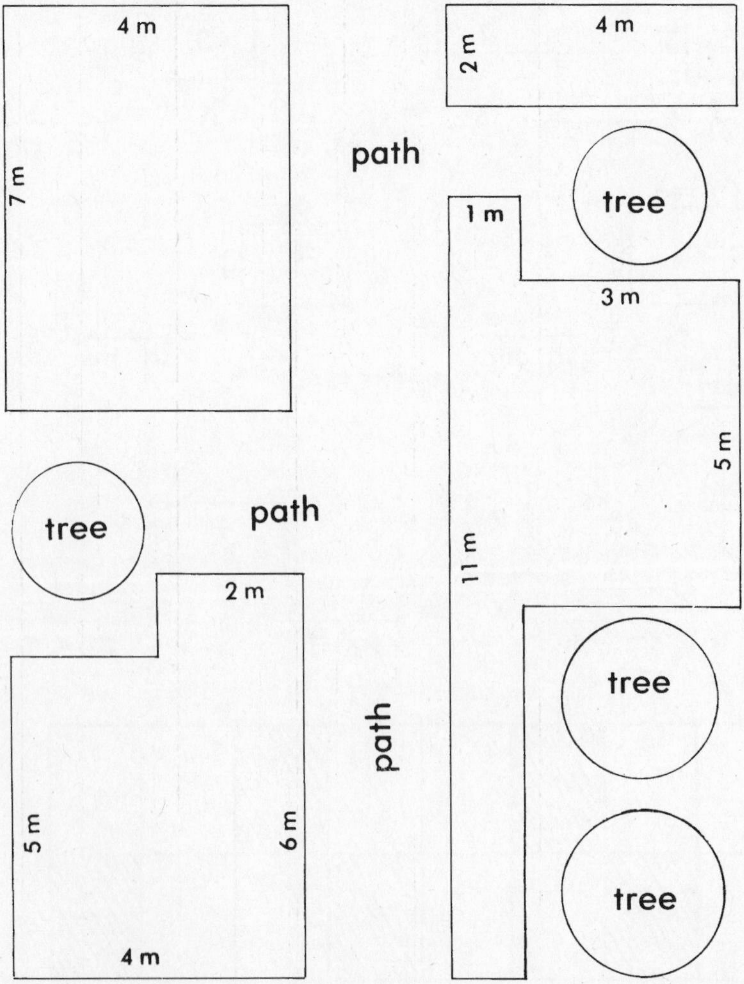

 0-88012-487-3

Area

Area (of a triangle) = ½(base × height)

$A = \frac{1}{2}(b \cdot h)$
$A = \frac{1}{2}(6\text{ cm} \times 3\text{ cm})$
$A = \frac{1}{2}(18\text{ sq. cm})$
$A = 9\text{ sq. cm}$

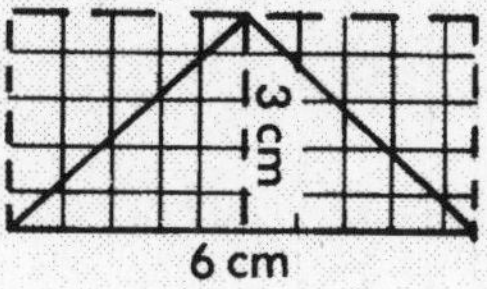

study this first

Find the area of each triangle.

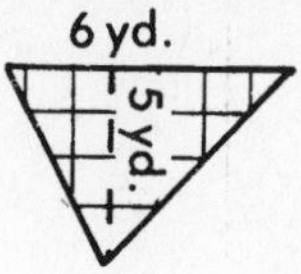

A =

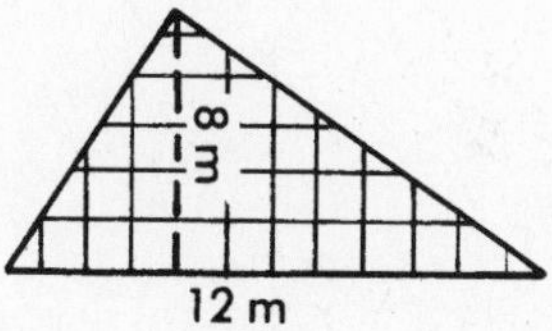

A =

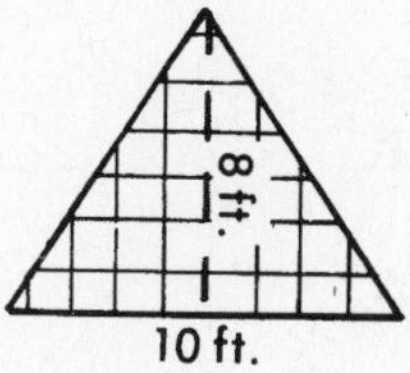

A =

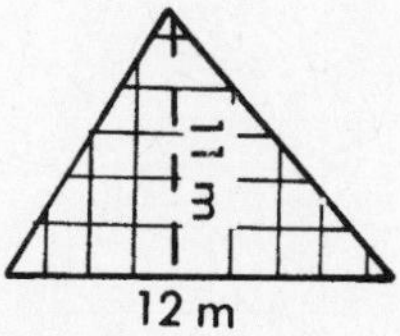

A =

0-88012-487-3

Area

Area (of a triangle) = ½ (base × height).

$A = \frac{1}{2}(b \times h)$

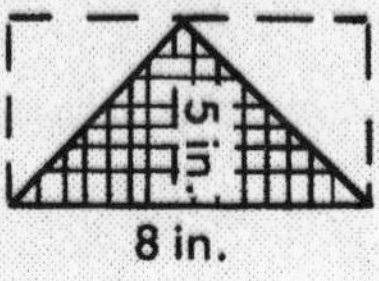

$A = \frac{1}{2}(8 \text{ in.} \times 5 \text{ in.})$

$A = \frac{1}{2}(40 \text{ sq. in.})$

$A = 20 \text{ sq. in.}$

Find the area of each triangle.

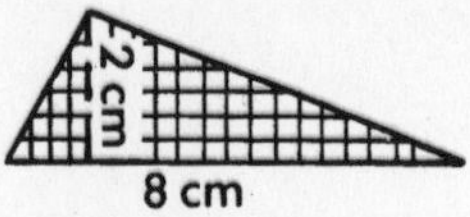

A =

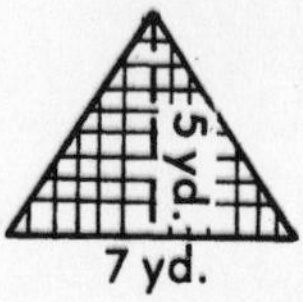

A =

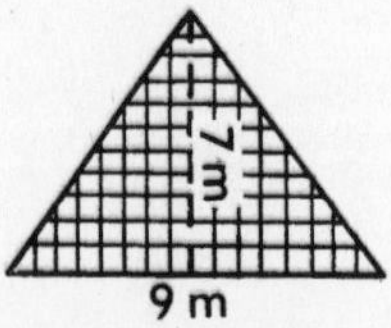

A =

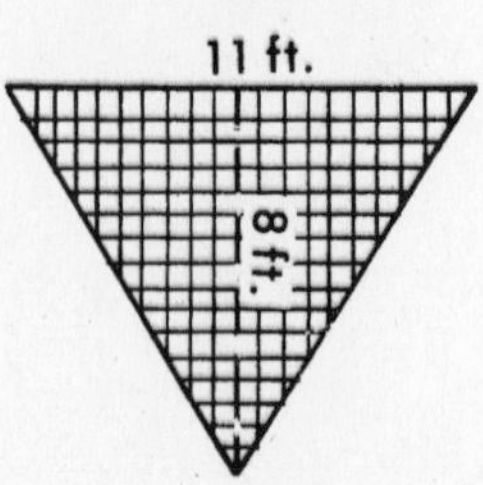

A =

0-88012-487-

Area

Area (of a parallelogram) = base × height.

$A = b \times h$

$A = (6\ m \times 3\ m)$

$A = 18$ sq. m

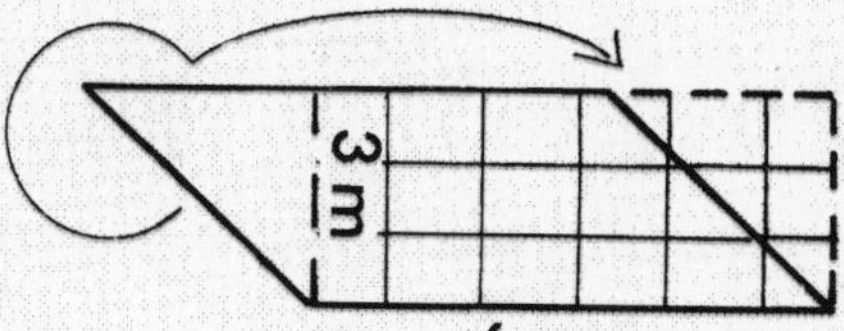

Find the area of each parallelogram.

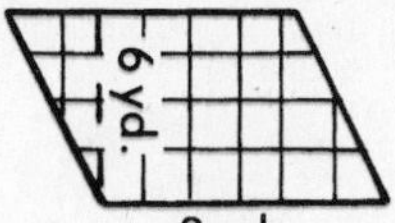

A =

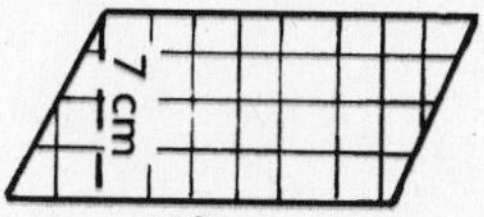

A =

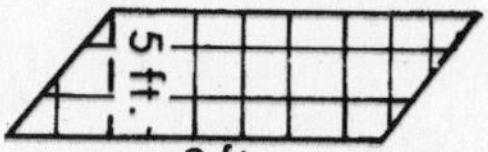

A =

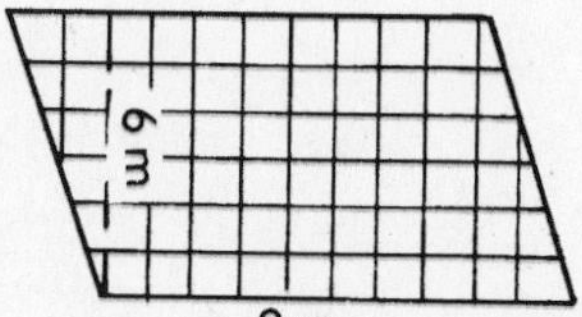

A =

0-88012-487-3

Area

Area (of a parallelogram) = base × height.

A = b × h

A = (8 in. × 4 in.)

A = 32 sq. in.

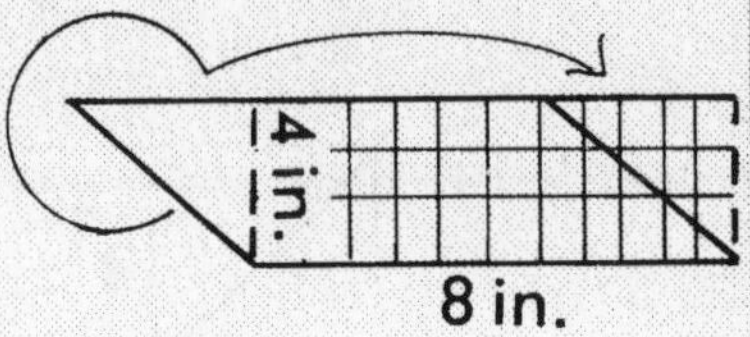

Find the area of each parallelogram.

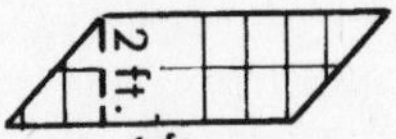

A =

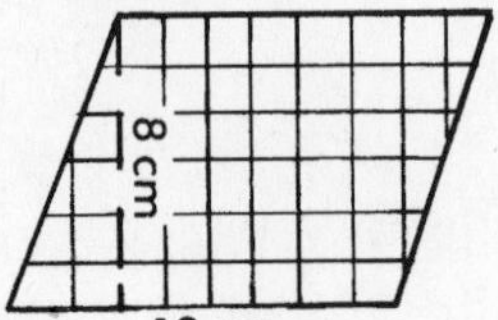

A =

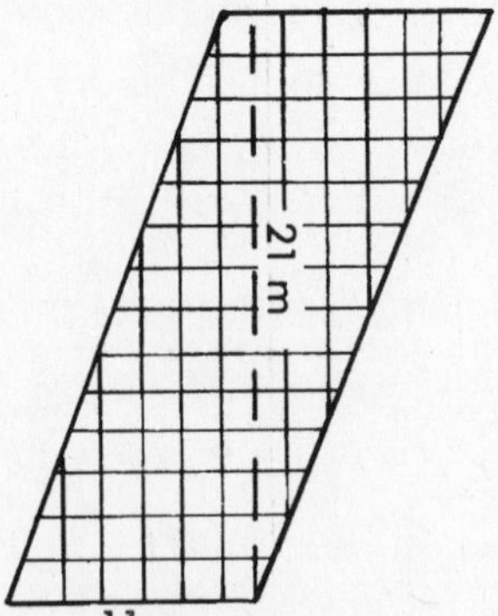

A =

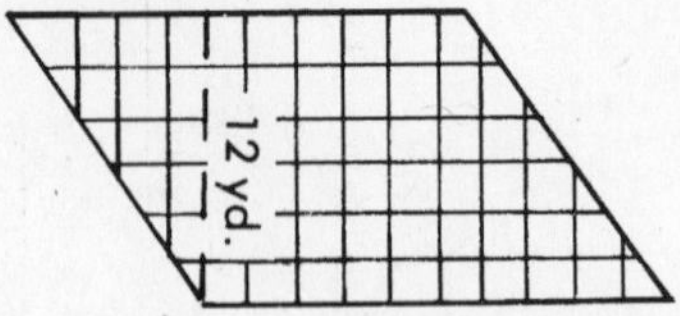

A =

 0-88012-487-

Area

Area (of a trapezoid) = ½(base + base′) × height

$$A = \frac{b + b'}{2} \times \frac{h}{1}$$

$$A = \frac{5\text{ cm} + 3\text{ cm}}{2} \times \frac{h}{1}$$

$$A = \frac{8\text{ cm}}{\not{2}_{1}} \times \frac{\not{2}^{1}\text{ cm}}{1}$$

$$A = 8\text{ sq. cm}$$

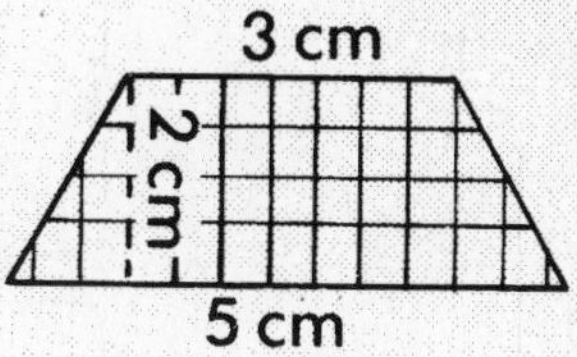

Find the area of each trapezoid.

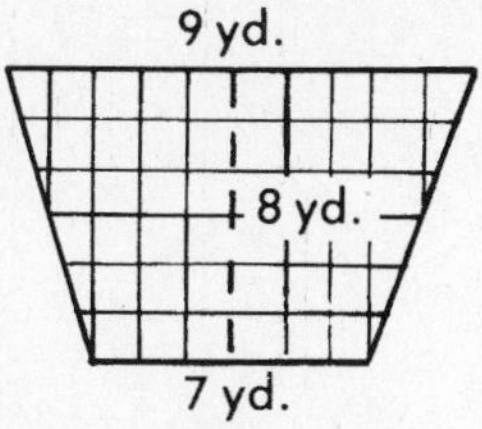

A =

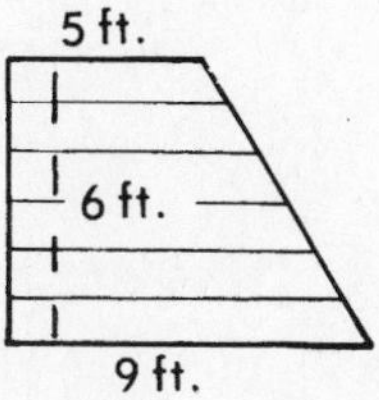

A =

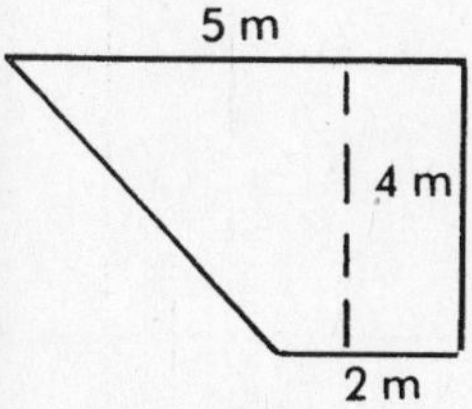

A =

0-88012-487-3

Area

Area (of a trapezoid) = ½(base + base′) × height.

$$A = \frac{b + b'}{2} \times \frac{h}{1}$$

$$A = \frac{4\text{ ft.} + 8\text{ ft.}}{2} \times \frac{5\text{ ft.}}{1}$$

$$A = \frac{12\text{ ft.}}{2} \times \frac{5\text{ ft.}}{1}$$

$$A = 6\text{ ft.} \times 5\text{ ft.}$$

$$A = 30\text{ sq. ft.}$$

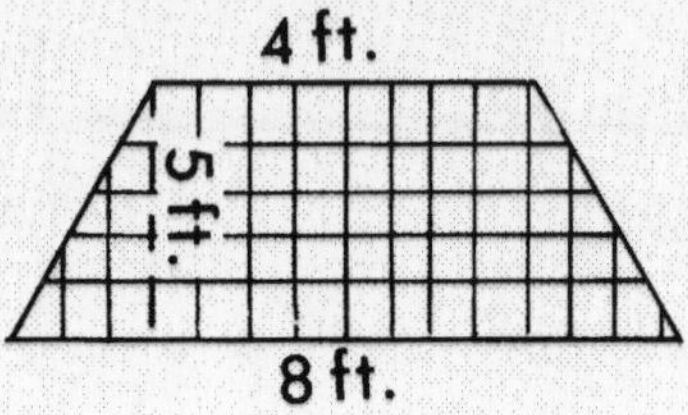

Find the area of each trapezoid.

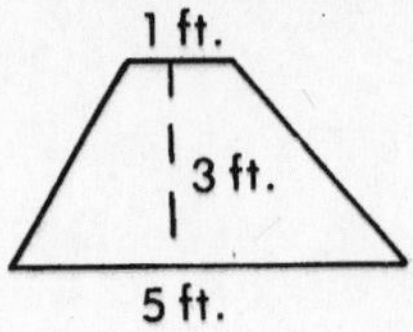

A =

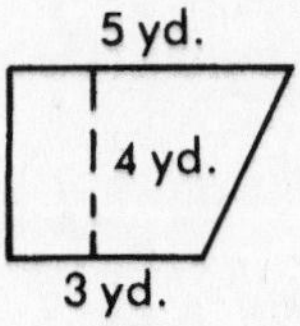

A =

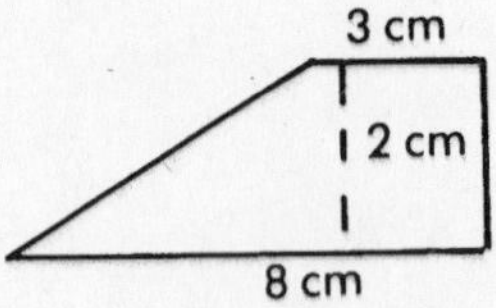

A =

0-88012-487-3

Area

Area (of a circle) $= \pi$ times the square of the radius.

$A = \pi r^2$

Let $\pi = 22/7$

$A = \frac{\overset{11}{\cancel{22}}}{\underset{1}{\cancel{7}}} \times \frac{\overset{1}{\cancel{7}}}{\underset{1}{\cancel{2}}}\,\text{cm} \times \frac{7}{2}\,\text{cm}$

$A = 77/2$ sq. cm

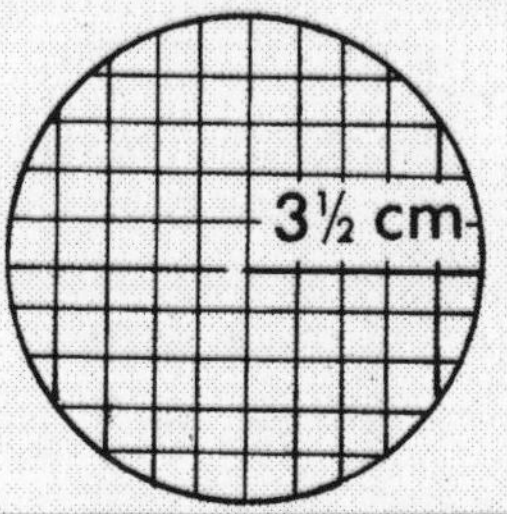

Your example

Find the area of each circle.

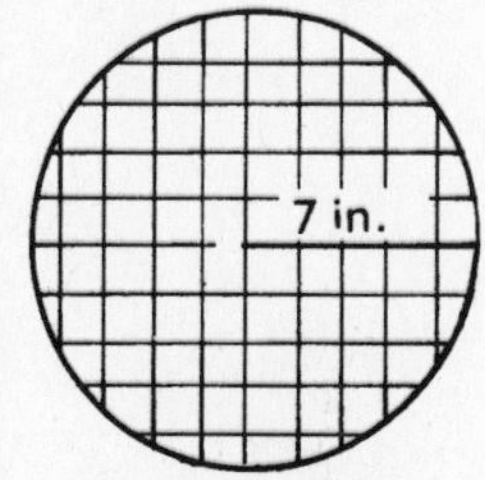

A =

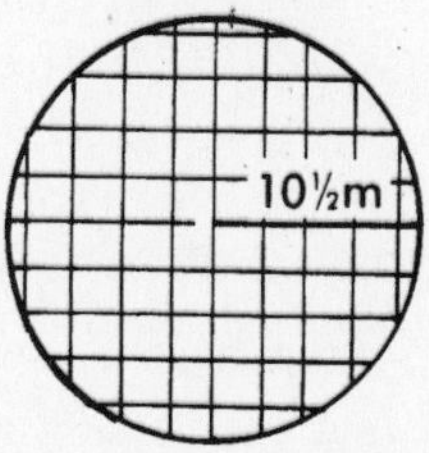

A =

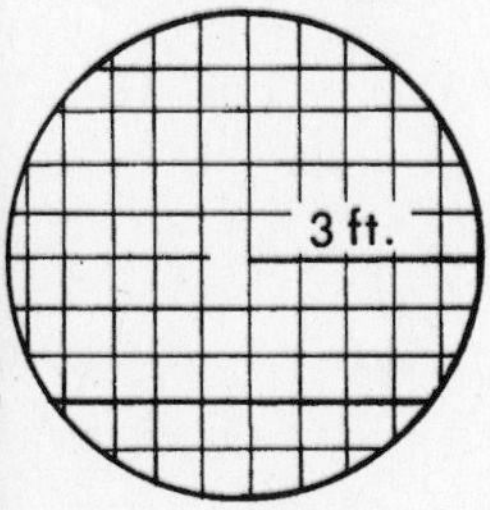

A =

0-88012-487-3

Area

Area (of a circle) = π times the square of the radius.

$A = \pi r^2$

Let $\pi = 3.14$

$A = 3.14 \times 7\text{ m} \times 7\text{ m}$

$A = 3.14 \times 49\text{ sq. m}$

$A = 153.86$

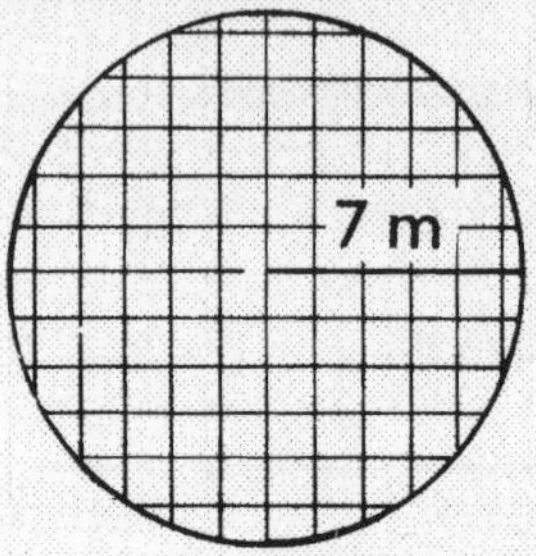

Find the area of each circle.

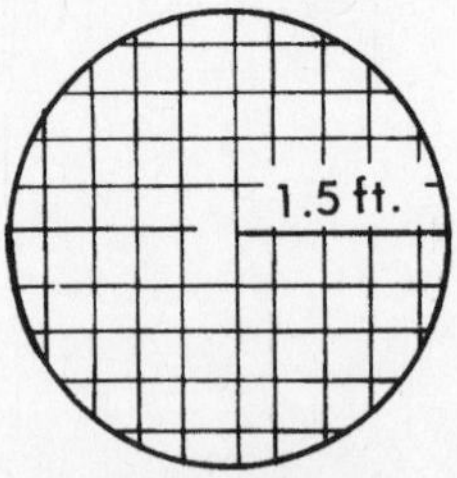

A =

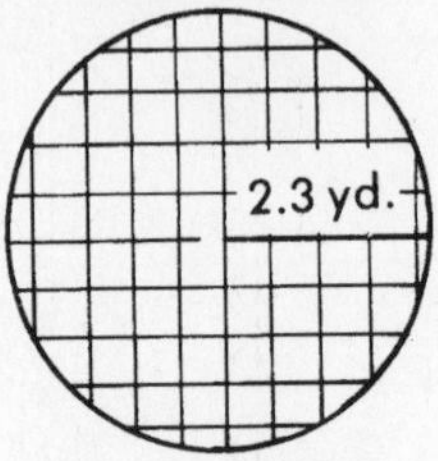

A =

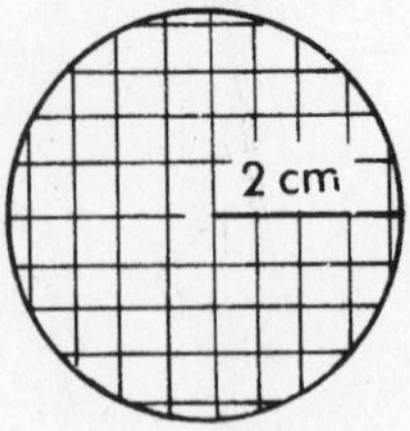

A =

0-88012-487-3